HIMALAYA: MOUNTAINS OF DESTINY

Landscape in Chitral in north-west Pakistan

HIMALAYA

MOUNTAINS OF DESTINY

WALTER LEIFER

TRANSLATED BY
URSULA PRIDEAUX

WITH 15 PAGES OF PLATES

LONDON: GALLEY PRESS LTD

Translated from the original text
Weltprobleme am Himalaya
published by Marienburg Verlag, Goettingen

CONTENTS

ILLUSTRATIONS

IT GIVES the author the greatest of pleasure to write his foreword
to the English version of a work concerned with the historical and
philosophical background of the political scene in the region centring on the Himalayas, for no European power has had so many
contacts with the area as Great Britain. It is worth drawing attention to one such contact at a surprisingly early date, during the
reign, in fact, of Alfred the Great of Wessex. This Anglo-Saxon
ruler sent a delegation of pilgrims to India, or vowed to do so, to
offer alms at the shrine of St Thomas at Mylapore. We read under
the date 883 in the Laud version of the *Anglo-Saxon Chronicle*:
'. . . and in the same year Sighelm and Aethelstan conveyed to
Rome, and also to India to St Thomas and St Bartholomew, the
alms which the King had vowed to send thither. . . .' This was in
fact a thank-offering for the recapture of the city of London from
the heathen Danes, against whom Alfred had invoked the inter-
cession of the two saints.

From then onwards the wheel of history begins to spin a thread,
tenuous but traceable in song and story and in the annals of pilgrimage, at first deeply imbued with the medieval dye of faith.
These pilgrims to India are a silent but explicit demonstration of
history. Not for six or seven centuries were they followed by
merchants from England. But in the steps of the merchants
pressed soldiers, administrators, adventurers and at last scholars.
And how vastly was the literature of Europe enriched when
Charles Wilkins translated the *Bhagavadgita*, the noble Song of
God, and William Jones first presented to the West the enchanting
story of Shakuntala which Goethe loved so much, and Colnebrooke,
Wilson, Woodroffe, Cunningham, Farquhar, Fergusson and so
many others devoted themselves to the new, exciting study of
Indian letters! The climax of this European science of Indology
is symbolized in the unique figure of Max Mueller, an Anglo-
German in the field of linguistics just as Handel is in the field of
music, and as eminent. Max Mueller laid the foundations, both
in literature and in pedagogy, of the present age of Indo-European
co-operation in all the arts and sciences. It was a long journey

from pilgrimage to partnership, and along the route lay adventure as well as humdrum administrative toil, commercial enterprise in widely dispersed trading factories despite all the blind alleys of ignorance and prejudice on either side.

Since my book first appeared in Germany, time has added a few more exciting scenes, set in the Himalayas, to the cosmic drama of history.

In March of 1959 the fourteen-year-old Dalai Lama fled from his palace at Lhasa, in order to escape on to Indian soil from the shame of being a crowned puppet and presiding over the mortal tragedy of his people. On the 17th of that month the population of Lhasa, followed by the rest of the Tibetan people, had risen, after the Dalai Lama had been summoned before the Chinese commandant and one of his palaces had been shelled. He followed the advice of his people to flee rather than be held as a pledge in pawn at the hands of the Chinese. Indian feeling was aroused and there was deep concern there about the temporal and spiritual head of Tibet and his people. Ever since the Dalai Lama had passed the Indian frontier post of Chutangmu in the North East Frontier Agency, on 31st March, he has been living in exile on the south-eastern slopes of the Himalayas, the fourteenth of the living incarnations of the Bodhisattva Avalokitesvara—and the silent, patient smile of a youth made wise by adversity still gives a glimmer of hope to the thousands of refugees from the high plateaux of the lamaseries. But in Tibet itself the too rapid destruction of the ancient social culture has plunged the people into confusion.

India, too, has suffered a shock from the flight of the Dalai Lama and the measures taken by the People's Republic of China against the Tibetan population, for the bonds between India and Tibet have been very close for untold ages through myth and religious usage, and now Tibet has been offered up on the altar of Indo-Chinese friendship. It was during the negotiations over Tibet that the five principles—the *Panch-Shila*—were first coined. Despite all the lip-service paid to them from Peking, those who sit in the seats of power in the Tien An Men, the political centre of Chinese Communism, have flagrantly violated the five principles and rendered them ineffective. The greatest political manifesto to come from the non-European world of our time has been treated by one of the contracting parties as nothing but a temporary demonstration.

Something new has been added also, from the moment when

Delhi was forced to announce to the world that the Chinese had attacked areas long looked on as Indian territory. The border regions of Ladakh, Spiti, Gahrwal and great sectors of the North East Frontier Agency were among the Himalayan areas occupied by China. White Papers and an uninterrupted exchange of Notes are the documentary evidence that the clouds over the Himalayas are a long way from dispersing yet. Chinese claims to the leadership of south-east Asia have been announced once before, in the era when Manchu China was dying, when K'ang-Yu-Wei published in his *Ta T'ung Shu* the future plans of Chinese world policy. This Chinese *Utopia* first saw the light in Darjeeling, the summer residence of the British rulers of Bengal; a Briton, Laurence G. Thompson, has quite recently published it in English. On 15th December 1939 Mao Tse-tung claimed back certain territories of south-east Asia for China in an article that has become notorious. K'ang's *Utopia* and Mao's demand still have their influence.

In the south, in the south-east and in the east of Asia, Chinese Marxism claims the lead in such a way as one day will brook no compromise. An event that roused echoes all over the world was the Indian action over Goa. Treaty relations between Portugal and Britain, derived from the Anglo-Portugese alliance of 1373, soon began to affect the Commonwealth relationship between Britain and India. And this was the moment that Pakistan chose to raise the question of Kashmir anew. But for India the wound along the MacMahon Line was more sensitive than ever. Before the forum of the United Nations dramatic events were played out. Their course is not nearly run yet, but they forced western statesmen and politicians to take more thought for the future of the world organization. It is rewarding to read in retrospect what Lord Home, then Foreign Secretary, said on 28th December 1961, and Harold Macmillan, Prime Minister, said on 5th February 1962, by way of careful analysis and admonitory, constructive criticism of the development of the United Nations, as they counted up the balance of the changes in the Himalayan region.

North of the Himalayas, above all, there is a perceptible disharmony between the two greatest Communist powers that almost rivals the world-wide conflict between East and West. On 9th September 1959 the Soviets announced through their press agency, *Tass*, that they deplored the Indo-Chinese 'incident', and two

years later to the day they took the opportunity, in the course of
the 'abandonment of the personality cult', to alter the name of
Mount Stalin, but, at the same time, they renamed another peak
'Mount Nehru'. This peak stands in their part of the Tien Shan
range along the Chinese border. However, despite such demonstrations, the Soviets cannot overcome Indian mistrust aroused by
the interpretation of the frontiers on Russian atlases.

Other recent events in the landscape of the gods and those who
seek them are dwarfed by the accumulated facts of history, but
even these few show that the political present with its sometimes
subtle, sometimes crude ramifications in all corners of the earth
is still preparing for us some surprises in the region of the
Himalayas, as elsewhere.

W. L.

April 1962.

1

Mythological Prologue

HOW GODS WERE FOSSILIZED IN THE MAJESTY OF THE MOUNTAINS

IT MAY be symbolic that the mountains, the highest and most powerful on our earth, which have become political and philosophical frontiers, are regarded by the people of their region as a unique creation. And furthermore, they themselves are, in the popular belief, holy and divine.

Those mountains which are gods, or in which the Divine is so powerfully and majestically demonstrated, this chain of ice-laden and snow-covered Himalayan heights, are thus stamped with the mark of the exceptional in the thoughts of their own sons and daughters.

The whole spiritual world of Hinduism is intent upon those hills and mountains of the Himalayas, which from time immemorial —who knows for how many thousands of years—have been the goal of pious pilgrimages and the scene of hard asceticism and ardent exercises.

In this region lies the holiest of all holy mountains, Kailas. How much inspiration has this mountain, by the sacred lake Mansarovar, given to Indian artists! How many known and unknown pilgrims were drawn through the Himalayan valleys to this place of pilgrimage on Tibetan soil, which, for men of the Sino-Tibetan and Indian culture, represents the geographical and spiritual heart of the Himalayas, where pious pilgrims at prayer are so near to the pulse of the Divine itself.

1

In a revered monument of Indian literature, the *Ramayana*, it is written:

When the earth of the Mansarovar region touches the body of any man, or when one bathes in this lake, the man shall enter the paradise of the Brahma, or he who drinks the water of the lake shall inherit Shiva's heaven. There is no mountain anywhere like the Himalayas, for there are Kailas and Mansarovar!

Kailas plays an important part not only in Hindu and Tibetan pilgrim lore, but also in the cosmogony of Hinduism. It lies upon the innermost of the seven great islands which form our world on Jambudwipa, and is called Mount Meru. Even if the interpretation of this mountain may be in part a different one, yet the identification of the earthly Kailas with the heavenly Meru is almost universal. Shiva's Kailas which stands upon the earth became the transcendence of Meru dedicated to Brahma, whose geographical position was as exactly determined to the north of the Himalayas as was that of Kailas.

The shape of Kailas has influenced the North Indian style of temple. People claim to rediscover the form of Shiva's mountain in the massive towers of the Hindu holy places. Kailas temples were built everywhere in order to carry the Himalayas into the smallest villages. Even the Buddhists, those stern reformers who in their original community banned every idol from their midst, succumbed to the myth of Kailas, and, in Central Indian Ellora, where they built a number of rock temples, have amongst other things also allowed a Hindu Kailas temple to be built in memory of Shiva's earthly palace. The Tamils call Mount Kailas the 'Northern Meru'. Standing on the roof of the great pagoda of Brihadiswara in Tanjore, in the state of Madras, a Brahmin pointed to the gilded monolithic block which forms the central tower over the sanctuary of the temple, and proudly explained to me: 'This is the Southern Meru. The power which goes forth from the holy mountain is effective here with us too.'

Mount Meru lies not only in heaven and on earth, but also in individual human beings. This philosophy is a piece of the Hindu view of totality. In the *Pretakalpa* of Garuda-Purana, in which we are given a statement of the Hindu cult of the dead and belief in the world to come—Emil Abegg translated it in 1921—is written in the fifteenth Adhyāya:

In the body as it is in reality are contained all worlds, mountains, continents and seas, the sun and the other constellations. . . . In the triangle [that is, the mystical region of the heart—Author] rises Mount Meru, in the lower corner the Mandara, in the right-hand corner the Kailāsa and in the left-hand corner the Himācala; on the upper side Nisadha, on the right-hand side Gandhamādana, and in the left-hand side Ramana: these are the seven mountains of the world.

A saying from the *Ramayana* is that he who but thinks of the Himalayas does greater things than he who is destined to tarry in Kashi, in Benares. Everyone knows of the sanctity ascribed to this place, today officially called Varanasi, by the Hindus and can therefore estimate the significance of the Himalayas for Indian culture. When Swami Vivekananda was once asked in the United States of America whether India's heat had not strongly influenced the form of the spiritual image of Hinduism, he replied that India's greatest spiritual possession had grown up not in the tropical climate of the Indian subcontinent but in the icy regions of the Himalayas, through the meditations of thinking and reflecting ascetics. Here in the regions where there are no more holy mountains than Mahadeo, Haramukh, Dhaulagiri and Annapurna, Badrinath and Kedarnath, Trishul and Nanda Devi—and above all, of course, Kailas—the snow-covered summits have always pointed to the highest, the inexplicable, the Divine. There can be no more beautiful sign of divinity than the royal mountain storming up to the clouds; indeed the gods themselves were frozen at the majesty of the clouds.

The tribute which poets paid to the holy mountain chain of the Himalayas can be only slightly indicated. Kalidasa, one of the masters, who knew how to set the well-formed Sanskrit words as a goldsmith sets precious stones, causes the Himalayas to rise up before us with supreme artistry. His *Meghaduta* ('Messenger of the Clouds') gives a survey of spiritual and geographical India. In it grandiose scenes are ever changing, and the pious Hindu will doubtless feel as he reads: Here I am actually in *Devabhumi*, in the 'land of the gods', as the Himalayan region has been called since Vedic times. In this work, on a journey through the ether which leads along the mythical routes from Ramagiri to the city of Alaka high up in the Himalayas, we learn of the individuality of all rivers which are traversed: Sipra, Vetravati, Nirvindhya, Narnawa and so on. They all offer so much material for the story-teller that they spread a gay-coloured carpet of legends before the listener or the reader. But then the messenger of the clouds comes near to the River Ganges, reverently called *Ganga* by Indian lips, into that Himalayan landscape which in the writings of Kalidasa is often called *Devatatma* ('Home of the Gods').

We may stop for a while at the Ganges because the thoughts and feelings of more than 300 million Hindus centre upon it. The Ganges, so runs an ancient legend, was the stream of heaven. Whoever speaks of it, of the event when the stream left the heavenly pastures, must begin with the story of King Sagara of Ayodhya. The latter once wanted to hold a horse sacrifice called *Asvanedha*, so as to become by this means lord of the countries, Chakravarti ('universal ruler'). But the god Indra jealously stole the sacrificial beast and sixty thousand descendants and relatives of Prince Ayodhya now sought the sacred horse all over the world. But when it seemed that they would soon discover it, Indra and his heavenly friends, who seemingly possessed many earthly vices, gave the alarm. They used their power to turn the sixty thousand suddenly to ashes. Then there was mourning in the royal house of Ayodhya. Wise Garuda, uncle of the slain, now announced that they would have to summon the heavenly stream of the Ganges down to earth, so as to carry away the ashes of the dead into the ocean of eternal peace. In the original tale two spiritual worlds clash: the more realistic Indoeuropean world, and the mentality of the oriental seekers after God, which is inclined to asceticism. As regards the Indoeuropean share in the story, let us recall that amongst one western branch, the Germanic tribes, a reminder of the old Aryan horse-worship is still kept alive in the coats of arms of Westphalia, Lower Saxony and Kent. But to return to the tale of the Ganges. Nobody was found able to perform the impossible task of fetching the Ganges down from Heaven except Bhagaritha, one of the blood relations of the slain. He tormented himself by self-martyr-dom and asceticism so much that the God Brahma himself had pity and promised the Ganges to the ascetic. In order to modify the downward rush of the river from Heaven, Shiva allowed it to be caught up by his eyebrow. Whereas we would speak of the labours of Hercules, in India people still speak today of a 'labour of Bhagaritha'. The story of the ascetic who brought the river of Heaven down to earth has much in common with the Hellenic tale of Sisyphus. But the Western encounter, born in constraint,

The Indus Valley

The Dalai Lama normally resides in this monastic palace, the Potala at Lhasa, capital of Tibet

has no success. In the oriental sphere, however, the stormer of Heaven, by prayer and voluntary self-torment, succeeds in converting the gods. Somewhere in the neighbourhood of Naini Tal in the Himalayas, when I heard of the Bhagaritha myth for the first time, the Brahmin interpreter of ancient Indian wisdom smiled at me and said: 'Is that not similar to the bidding of Christ to ask and to knock again and again until God's door is opened to the human suppliant?'

Swami Sivananda, of the Yoga-Vedanta-Wood University of Rishikesh on the River Ganges, the creator of the Hindu Divine Life Society, founded in 1936, and one of the most frequently sketched personalities of spiritual India, today carries the religious message of the Himalayas beyond the boundaries of his native land. In a pilgrim's book which Swami Sivananda published, we find the interpretation of a pilgrimage to the most sacred piece of earth in our world, as a Hindu sees it:

If you have happily survived an arduous pilgrimage, you are not to forget that the fruit of such a pilgrimage is not by any means the pleasure of having seen the heights of Kailas or having bathed in Mansarovar or Gauri Kund, or of having encountered unforgettable scenery on the journey. Nothing of the kind! Here in the holy region of Kailas and Mansarovar you are surrounded by a holy atmosphere. Seize the golden opportunity. In the morning and the evening, if not all day long, seek out for yourselves a place in silent contemplation of the divinity which lies there before you in the form of holy Kailas and Lake Mansarovar. Then surrender yourselves there to meditation, in order to rise to the highest peaks of spirituality and to make your hearts as pure as the snow which covers the peak of Kailas and your mind as crystal clear and transparent as the waters of Mansarovar. Then all the impurities in your hearts and spirits will fall from you.

At this point I may perhaps indicate that in the whole Western world—largely thanks to the Indian Divine Life Society, which has a strong influence abroad—there are great numbers of people who also pay homage to the myth of the Himalayas. In our own time there has spread an orientalism which attracts certain Western circles more and more strongly, and so it is not surprising that such ideas are today presented by a Swiss woman, Margarete Schneider, in various journals such as *Voice of the Himalayas* or *Synthèse Universelle* published from Geneva. For this European woman Swami Sivananda is 'the Towering Saint of the Himalayas'.

This is the name, too, of a publication in which she pointed to the influence of the Swami.

The whole of the Himalayas is sacred to the Hindus and they are personified in the mystical form of Himavan. But Himavan's daughter is Uma-Parvati, the wife of Shiva, whom we in Europe often call, by way of simplification, the destroyer, beside Brahma, the creator, and Vishnu, the preserver. Of all the Hindu gods, Shiva has probably the largest number of worshippers. The Shiva philosophy has also greatly enriched Hindu literature. The mystical element is especially represented in this philosophy. However, many Europeans are repelled by the symbol of Shiva, the phallus, called *lingam* in India, which dates back to the era of a primitive religion. But the disciple of Shiva will stress the symbolic meaning. It is to him the immediate proof that Shiva preserves the creative element in himself. Everything created is said to have been born out of chaos, and the god whose name means 'good omen' to provide the cause for this. There are differing opinions amongst Indian scholars and Brahmins as to when the worship of Shiva began. There is no doubt that a god of this name did not exist in Vedantic times, yet the old Indoeuropean god Rudra was probably his prototype, and to this were attributed more and more characteristics and symbols of non-Indoeuropean gods, until the name of the god was changed too.

But the Himalayas do not belong only to Shiva. The descendants of Shiva are of course also inseparable from the holy mountain range: Ganesh, the god with the elephant's trunk, who bestows wisdom and happiness, and Kartikkeya, who is called on in time of war. The latter is generally called Skanda or Subrahmanya in southern India. The heavenly generalissimo usually rides upon a peacock. Therefore it is not for nothing that this bird is sacred amongst the warlike race of Rajput, and may not be shot in the territory of the present-day Indian republican state of Rajasthan.

Brahma and Vishnu, who, in contrast to the eternal wanderer Shiva, reign in the divine halls, have their relationship to the Himalayas. I will mention only one of the many stories: how a fish, who was the incarnation—*avatara*—of Vishnu, saved Manu from the waves of the all-destructive Great Flood. The cosmic disaster —called the Flood by Christians—which once deposited Noah's Ark in the safety of Mount Ararat, with species of all the different kinds of animals, has a parallel in the Hindu world, which, exactly as in the case of Hebrews, Babylonians, Hellenes and many other races, keeps alive the remembrance of a world cataclysm. The Himalayas became the saving mountain of Lomonoras, and the Indian Noah, Manu—the man—along with his seven *Rishis*, or priestly scholars, who sat with him in the boat drawn by the divine fish, gave to the world a new order. Manu's words, the law of the Himalayas, written upon the peaks of the divine mountains, are still respected today as the original law in the land of India. Moreover, many Indian writings also call Brahma the god who hid himself in the body of a fish, in order to save the human race. In all the ancient myths, however, the one theme echoes: at some time or other an epoch of world history must have been ended by a great natural catastrophe.

In addition to the tale of the flood, the story of the building of the Tower of Babel had its Himalayan parallel. The Austrian-born Himalayan researcher, René von Nebusky-Wojkowitz, has written of it in his work *Where Gods are Mountains*. He recounts that in ancient times a branch of the Lepcha race, called the Naong, decided to build a high tower. When the people who were building the top of the tower called to the helpers to bring grappling irons with them in order to seize heaven, the calls were misunderstood on earth. They thought that the news was being passed down from the top of the tower that heaven had already been reached. Thereupon they pulled away the main supports and the tower collapsed. But those people who were able to save themselves from the disaster suddenly noticed that they did not understand each other any more and that each one spoke a different language. That is the story of the individualization of the human race handed down by a tiny Himalayan tribe. Matthias Hermanns also tells the story in his work on the Indo-Tibetans.

The holy mountains are alive not only in Hindu mythology; in Tibetan culture they have also been sources of religious inspiration and literary fantasy. In Tibetan language there are two versions of the *Kang-ri Karchhak*—these are the Tibetan *Kailasa Puranas*, those Hindu tales which grow around the holy mountain and which in Buddha's country were adapted for lamaistic readers. In *Kang-ri Karchhak* one can read that Mount Kailas—the Tibetans call it Kang Ringpochhe—is the centre of the universe. Lamaistic Buddhism, this extraordinary mixture of ancient

B

faith in the gods and of the teaching of Buddha which is unfavour-
able to everything metaphysical and divine, names Demchhok as
the divine protector of Kailas. His other name is Pavo. This god
Demchhok is wrapped in a tiger skin and round his neck he wears
a sinister chain of human skulls. In addition he carries *damaru*,
the trumpet, and *bhatam*, the trident. The divine emblems show
the relationship of Demchhok to the pair of Hindu gods Shiva—
Parvati. Amongst the Hindus, when the destructive feminine
power in her is seen, the divine wife Parvati bears, however, the
name Durga or Kali. The spouse of the god Demchhok is Dorje-
Phangmo. In the Indian sphere her name is Vajra-Varahi. Demchhok was, of course, not on Kailas but on the peak of Tijing. Kailas,
reserved, according to the Hindus, for Shiva and his spouse is,
in the Tibetan view, inhabited by Buddha and five hundred
Bodhisattvas. These *Bodhisattvas* are beings who were on the way
to the state of Buddha, but have renounced it in order to redeem
other men.

It will cause no surprise that the Tibetans make pilgrimages
to and around their most sacred mountain just as the Hindus do.
A day's pilgrimage of this kind is called *parikrama* by the Indians
and *ningkor* by Tibetans. Just as the Tibetans, in their lamaistic
teaching, often show a road to salvation in the plainest and
simplest manner—namely, in the recitation of magic formulae
and in the turning of holy words by means of prayer mills—so
there is too for the wealthy people of the country a convenient
way of relieving oneself from an arduous pilgrimage. The journeys
around Kailas or a pilgrimage around Mansarovar—Tso Mapham
or Tso Mavang as they are called by the sons of the country—one
can have carried out by servants or beggars, in exchange for an
adequate payment and provisioning. When he can show 108
pilgrimages, the pious Hindu is certain of *Mukhta*, the highest
grace of god, and the Tibetan is certain of *Nirvana*, release from
all suffering.

It may cause surprise that not only do the Tibetan lamaistic
books honour the lake and the mountain as the sacred centres of
the land of Buddha, but that even the Buddhist writings in Pali
and Sanskrit mention them. In this literature Mansarovar bears a
significant second name: *Anotatta*, or *Anavatapta-lake*, without
heat or unrest. This Anavatapta is paradise upon earth. Here
lotus flowers bloom and royal swans—*rajahansas*—sail along

majestically between them. Kailas and Mansarovar in the divine garden of Shiva are accessible only to the person who is meditating. The sceptical son of the West will find a gloomy Tibetan inland lake and behind it one of the many mountains of the roof of the world, which to be sure tower up much higher and more regally in the actual Himalayas.

It should also be mentioned here that in Persia, Afghanistan, China and Burma, the Himalayas and their most holy places penetrated into the literature, that they inspired the peoples of south-east Asia in exactly the same way and that, from Laos and Cambodia to Indonesian Bali, they are buried as deeply in the consciousness of the people as in parts of the Himalayan region itself. The Himalayan myth has transformed Buddhism in these territories, and lamaistic Buddhism, which is predominant amongst Tibetans, Mongolians and Kalmuks, is also called *Vajrayana*— the diamantine vehicle. The two other large groups of world Buddhism are 'the large vehicle', *Mahayana*, the Chinese-East Asiatic species, and 'the small vehicle', *Hinayana*, the branch of the belief found in Ceylon, Burma, Laos, Thailand and Cambodia.

Even the Jains, that Indian religious community which seeks salvation without the help of priests or of the Brahmin gods, did not free itself from the spiritual pressure of the Himalayas. In their works they call Kailas *Ashtapada* and Mansarovar *Padma Hrada*. Those great saints of Jainism, the *Tirthankaras* or preparers of fords, begin with Adinatha Vrishabhadeva, who attained his *Nirvana*, his final release from the suffering of wandering from rebirth to rebirth.

The myth of the Himalayas is an endless coil. Thousands of years have helped to wind it, and Sadhus and Swamis are still meditating in the icy deserts—men who always wear the pilgrim's garment of the priestly beggars of Hinduism.

These wise men stand meditating in the Himalayas as frontier guards of spiritual India. No record shows what low temperatures they endure there and how high they climb—and, goodness knows, it is as well that Western sensationalism still pauses before these silent men. One of these Hindu pilgrims once told me that in the Himalayas, in the midst of a nature which is completely deified, one can only draw near to what is 'placeless', the really divine spot, if one thinks away beyond all that which is too deeply rooted in mythology and tries only to trace the original divinity. One must throw the gods overboard. I interposed to ask whether Buddha had not done that and whether Buddhism, and what is known as Buddhism today, did not just show that certain limits might not be crossed.

My contemplative friend replied that those who were drawing near to the deity did not just cross that frontier because they were bidding farewell to thousands and thousands of gods but not to the great nameless deity. 'And those men over there'—he pointed to the Himalayan peaks—'go even further, and even want to banish from our minds that nameless thing which we worship in silence. Yet the soul and the faith of the Himalayas are stronger. . . .'

Beyond the Himalayas new gospels are being proclaimed. In the greatest of the Slav empires and in the most powerful of the Sino-Asiatic realms, these new prophets are at work. And the patriarch of a new generation of materialistic prophets is a German Jew from Trier, the ancient city on the Moselle. But this gospel teaches that Paradise can be found in a different way, in fact already here on earth, and not through meditation, prayer and asceticism.

To its children the mountains of the Himalayas are gods. Was that why the Soviet Russians changed the name of Pamir's Mount Everest, Kauffmann Peak (formerly named after a German governor of tsarist Turkestan) to Lenin Peak and Garmo to Stalin Peak? In many places in the *Rig-Veda* one can read this sentence: 'Kasyeme himavanto mahitva sam no adri sam no parvatah.' ('These great Himalayan mountains are a most significant omen for us.')

This sentence, which thousands of years ago had a religious meaning, today suddenly receives a burning political reality.

Historical Prelude

NOT only devout pilgrims, enraptured poets and philosophers were drawn to the mountainous land of the gods. Leaders of different expeditions gazed towards the lands around 'Devabhumi'. Their aims were more 'realistic', and changed from century to century.

From the sterile plains of the north, peoples were always attracted to districts which promised riches and well-being. Bold tribes won empires and thrones for themselves. Thus there arose, to the south of the Himalayas, kingdom after kingdom, founded by wave after wave of new conquerors.

Over and above that, the Central Asian area—known to professional historians as *vagina gentium*, 'the womb of the nations'—has given to the world an unheard-of political task. The Central Asian nomad began the attack upon the city civilizations in the river regions of Europe and Asia. The world to the north of the Himalayas was constantly in a state of disintegration. For hundreds of years this world was 'Asia' to Europeans. But the real Asia consists of the old civilizations: from Arabia, the Iranian bridge to India, and from there stretching to Indo-China, where the Indian and Chinese cultural spheres meet; from there the paths lead to Indonesia and to the spiritual kingdom of the Far East.

All these ancient cultures contrast with the parched steppes of Central Asia, where hunger and poverty always shadowed the mounted tribes.

11

We do not know when the urge to wander seized the peoples of Central Asia for the first time in history. North of the Himalayas, in the wide landscapes of the steppes and deserts, were territories, first of hunting, then of stock-breeding clans. Cattle and sheep were their favourite animals—in northern Asia it was the reindeer. But the horse became the noblest of all domestic animals. The Turks were probably the first people to ride upon horseback. This period of world history in which the breeding of horses played a large part originated between the mountains of Altai and Abakan. In the cultivation and preservation of fodder, and in the organization of hunting expeditions, these equestrian tribes learnt how to form a closely organized society. Here in the Turanian territory of the great Himalayan region there grows the cultural circle of the patriarchal riders who gradually developed from hunters to breeders. The rise of countries devoted to horse-breeding, in the region which has its axis in the Himalayas, is the dynamic force in an encounter between northern Asia and the ancient civilized lands which lasted for many thousands of years.

Just as the patriarchal horsemen, lords and rulers, originated to the north-west of the Himalayas, so the matriarchal collectors of berries, who developed into cultivators of plants, had their original home in the south-east of the divine mountain range. There in the jungle valleys from Assam to Annam, where the ever-open sluice gates of heaven produce luxuriant tropical vegetation in stark contrast to the patriarchal lands, the culture centring on the law of the mother had one of its beginnings. Women and princesses—mothers—ruled here. Village culture, proceeding from the community of women, here becomes the basis of the social constitution, in contrast to the large sphere of endeavour of the herdsmen and stock-breeders, who, on their horses and camels, had to seek out whole empires in order to find food for their herds. And the original faith in a higher being developed differently amongst the breeders of herds and the cultivators of plants. One experiences God more deeply and clearly in steppes and deserts. When there are a number of gods, one supreme god rules at the same time in highest heaven, whilst the chattering and planting mothers tell of demons and spirits under the palm trees. The male enlightenment of the north-west is cut off from the female obscurity in the south-east—and the divine Himalayas, impassable, unconquerable until Europe's sons came, lie like a mighty arch between the sites of two ancient cultures which survived and intermingled in a thousand variations.

Then, out of the mists of primeval times, there echo the first names of the races which stepped into the dawning light of history.

In the Indian sphere, the remains of Mohenjo-Daro and Harappa still pose problems for historians and archaeologists. The seals which were found in 1922, and later in the mud of the Indus countryside, have still not been deciphered, and their creators are therefore unknown. Were they Aryans, Dravidians or members of other races? Until then it was believed that the Dravidians and the Austro-Asiatic Munda peoples in the Indian subcontinent were the original inhabitants of the country. The explorer Fürer-Haimendorf propounded the thesis of a migration of Dravidians from the west.

The inhabitants of Mohenjo-Daro had active relationships with the West. In the ruined cities of Mesopotamia Indus clay tablets were found which can be dated to approximately the time between 2700 and 2600 B.C. In the surviving diplomatic correspondence in tiles dating from the fourteenth century B.C., between the Upper Asian kings of the Hittites and the Mitanni, Shuppililiuma and Mattiwaza, many Indo-Aryan gods are mentioned. Here the Indian Nasatyas appear under the name of Nasattiyanna. That may mean that either the Aryans in the year 1360 B.C. had already been long established in north-west India, or that they lived in Asia Minor, ready to march on towards the East.

The Indians could have learnt from their Chinese neighbours just what the precise dating of historical facts means. However since they prefer to clothe history in the garments of mythology we must trace these myths back to their historical kernel. The best source for research into Indo-Aryan primeval times is the epic *Mahabharata*, which tells of the struggle between the two branches of the moon dynasty, the *Kuru* and the *Pandu*. These battles took place in the Ganges-Jumna region, which is still today the political centre of India. The Bharata tribe—their king Sudas might well be one of the first historically identifiable personalities of India—later gave the land its name. In the eastern territory of Aryavata, of Aryan India, the kings of the Sun dynasty created kingdoms for themselves in Kosala and Videha. One of them, Rama, later received divine honour as a reincarnation of Shiva.

To the north of the Himalayas, in the world of China, in the land of *Sinanthropus pekinensis*, Chinese culture makes its entry into history. An older culture proceeds from Shansi, Honan, Kansu and Shensi: the Yang-shao culture, well known for its painted ceramics. Somewhat later—about 2000 B.C.—we find the Lung-shan culture, extending from Chekiang to Shantung, characterized by ceramic of a single colour, black or grey. The surprising thing is that Western research workers see the starting-point of this Lung-shan culture in the countryside of West Turkestan.

From the clash of those ancient cultures in the limestone areas by Hwang-ho and Yang-tse Kiang there arose the Middle Kingdom. It is the kingdom which, built into the cultural framework of Confucius, gives a complete form to ceremonial, to a polished way of life, to the status of cultured men of letters and scholars competing in the written word. In this state, which believes itself to be the centre of the world, everything is reduced to an order (the saving strength of which is Tao) which reflects the cosmos and the rule of the lord of heaven, Shang-ti, upon earth.

In the northern sky there hangs the motionless Pole Star. It is the pole of heaven, the symbol of divine fullness of power. The Chinese looked towards the north because that was the direction of the highest lord of heaven. It was not for nothing that the earthly representatives of the lord of heaven on China's imperial throne, the 'Sons of Heaven', lived for long in the northern city, Peking. They dreamed their dreams from there, they and their political successors, who put into their state coat of arms the imperial palace *Tien An Men* ('The gate of heavenly peace'), and above it, in a group of five stars, one—like the Pole Star—which shines brighter and stronger than the others.

New names resounded in the western approaches of the Himalayas when Zarathustra proclaimed from Bactria to the people of Iran his passionate gospel of the divine lord Ahura Mazda and his devilish counterpart Ahriman. Spiritual Persia-Iran was rising resplendent in the Orient. Its torch was not to be extinguished when the Macedonian Alexander entered upon the inheritance of the great Persian kings, who proudly called themselves 'kings of Asia'. The light of this torch received a new and remarkable glow when the fire cult of the Zoroastrian religion was united with the teaching of the god Mithras. And later Persia spoke a different language in the world of Islam—that of the Protesters or Shiites.

The Macedonians were on the march—Alexander's most

successful gift to Asia was this: Bactria, wish-child of an Indo-Iranian-Hellenistic synthesis.

The spiritual heritage of the Hellenes was nurtured on the banks of the Indus and the Oxus. The language of Athens flowered in the kingdoms which climbed up to the Himalayas from the west.

But in that area in which a synthesis of European and Asiatic culture was completed, uniting the Persian, Indian and Hellenistic strains, there came about also a syncretism which blended ideas and at the same time strove to rise above religions. Europe and Asia were never closer than in the Greek 'moment' of the epoch after Alexander. The political trend was from west to east, but the religious waves flowed in the opposite direction. Thus Christianity, too, turned across the Mediterranean towards Europe, and its main missionary activities were not directed towards the east. For that reason its centres are to be found at the outposts of the old Roman republic, and not in the places of the Achaemenidian empire, from which, it is true, a branch of Christianity, the Nestorian sect, tried later to convert the Indoeuropean and Mongolian peoples. Mighty rulers of the race of Genghis Khan listened with tolerance and respect to these missionaries of the Christian faith.

While Zarathustra was completing his work of reform in Iran, Siddhartha Gautama, the Buddha, attacked Hinduism, which was proliferating in the jungle of the gods. He was the great negative thinker, who fought against the hierarchic world of the Brahmins, and adapted himself in his missionary work to the social and cultural situation of the times. Out of the dynamic of Buddha's missionaries, which was in complete contrast to the doctrine which they proclaimed, there proceeded from the Himalayas, where the historic Buddha was born in what is now Nepal, a religious movement which is still widespread today in eastern Asia, in the Tibetan-Mongolian regions, in south-east Asia and Ceylon, and which has left behind marked traces even in present-day Hinduism. Amongst the foreign influences to which Buddhism was exposed belongs in particular a Greek-Buddhist synthesis which gives a universal significance to the doctrine of the king's son from the Himalayan race of the Sakya, which today appears as a markedly Asiatic doctrine. And finally, it was the 'Constantine of Buddhism', the Emperor Asoka, who translated into the Indian the conception of the religious world ruler, called Chakravarti by the philosophers of India, which belongs more to upper Asia, and thus, from the Himalayan kingdom of the Maurya, proclaimed a policy which after bloody experiment renounced force and pledged itself to tolerance and peace. With Asoka, India began to play an active part in world politics.

Today, in the twentieth century, when there is much talk in evangelical Christian circles of freeing religion from mythology, one may well say that Buddha is the first person known to us to have preached the same doctrine twenty-five centuries ago.

From the Himalayas, too, Vardhamana Mahavira proclaimed his message of Jainism, which in ethics covers almost the same ground as Buddhism, but in questions of asceticism, observance of the cult and in the doctrine of the immortality of souls is again as far removed from it. The Jainist conception of *Ahimsa* was strongly defined, and carried with it the prohibition against killing any living being.

India's history has run through many kingdoms and dynasties. Few of them are so brightly inscribed in the book of history as Magadha, the great Indian kingdom of Maurya, or the Sung dynasty. Added to these are the kingdoms of the Greeks in the Punjab and also the states of Ksatrapa, Kerala, Chola Pandya and Gupta.

From the first century before Christ, India sensed a new world beating at its gates. The Huns of Central Asia had driven the Yüeh-chih out of what is now Turkestan. These people may be the Indoeuropean Tokhars who in their turn drove out the equally Indoeuropean Saka from their Central Asiatic homeland. The Yüeh-chih established themselves in Bactria, the Saka in what is today northern Pakistan. Thus the steppes announced their arrival at India's ancient point of invasion.

It became a matter of pressure and counterpressure between the races of the steppes and the civilized nations. As early as 750 B.C. the Scythians threatened what is now Russia from what is now Turkestan. They encountered a Thracian-Phrygian race, which now in its turn approached related peoples of Asia Minor for help. Thus the expedition of the Scythians had reached the arena of world politics. The empire of the Persians was given the alert. The Scythian expeditions were now amongst the obvious military and political measures taken by the great Achaemenidian kings.

In the third century B.C. the Sarmatians burst forth from the region of Lake Aral, to occupy the present-day southern Russian provinces. At the same time, in the Orchon territory, the ancient centre of the Mongolian races, a clan (the Hsiung-nu) had united all the Turkish and Mongolian races and for the first time was threatening China. The unifier of the Middle Kingdom, the first emperor with the title Shih-Huang-ti, thereupon gave the order to build, out of the small frontier fortresses against the races of the steppes, the mighty Great Wall, the forerunner of the Roman Limes, of the Maginot Line and of what is probably the last military fortification of the modern world constructed in the traditional military spirit, the Atlantic Pact. One of the Tokharian tribes, the Kushan, founded in northern India a powerful dynasty, called Kusana by the Indians, which promoted Sanskrit and was favourable to Buddhism and opened up for it, through the connection of its ruling house with Central Asia, a way to the interior of the continent. At the same time the Graeco-Bactrian and Graeco-Indian kingdoms were dissolved and the Iranian and Hellenistic cultural influences were blended with the Indian ones. Such was the result of the penetration of the Huns from Central Asia!

The cultural, political and social conditions of the Iranian-North Indian and Turkestan areas changed quickly. Meanwhile Western and Eastern Huns marched farther and farther. China's military leaders adapted themselves to the tactics of the steppes, did away with the slow battle chariot and formed a cavalry force after the model of the races of the steppes. Yet the threat from the steppes remained. Huh-nan-yeh, Chih-chih, Mo-yung, Toba, are the names of some of these peoples of the steppes, who gazed, hungry for land, over the cultivated landscape of China.

In the third century after Christ the Huns were on the march again. Liu-Ts'ung was the name given by the Chinese to the Hun conqueror of northern China, who captured two of their emperors and had them hanged. At the same time the Huns pressed forward on the other front towards the West, and put the great south Russian empire of the Goths, once established by Ermanarich, into a state of dissolution, thereby arousing terror amongst the East Germanic tribes. The latter moved out towards the West. With this event the Migration of the Peoples, which, as our history books inform us, began in about A.D. 375 but in reality had been an ever-recurring event for a thousand years, a periodical invasion of the people of the steppes into the areas of city culture, now includes also the Germanic-Romance region of Europe. The Germanic kingdoms founded in the western Roman territory had, because of the pressure of other races from the region, originated to the north and north-west of the Himalayas. The Germanic peoples were not the usurpers but the usurped. In the person of Attila, the entire shadow of the Asiatic middle region of the steppes was thrown across Europe, and the western *Imperium Romanum* broke up. The tragedy of the Nibelungs pervaded the whole continent. A hundred years later Mahirakula, who bore the title of 'Attila of India', rode out against the cities of northern India. His wild riders shattered the framework of these regions. The warrior caste of Gujerat today still traces its descent back to these riders.

In the sixth century, when internal tribal warfare in the original Central Asian home of the Huns drew attention to new tribes, the Kao-ch'üeh or Tolos and the T'u-chüeh, we have to deal with the entry of the Uzbek and Turkish peoples into history. This is, moreover, the moment for China to take possession of the Tarim basin and to destroy the remains of Indoeuropean culture there. Fifteen centuries later philologists are again taking an interest in these most north-easterly of Aryan dialects, which we now know under the collective name of Tokharian.

Meanwhile another race appeared upon the scene to the west of the Himalayas: the Arabs, driven by the dynamism of Mohammed's teaching. With Chinese aid, through internal strife, the Turkish Uighurs had made themselves the leading tribe. However, the Arab attack, against which both Chinese and Uigurs turned, decided the future of Turkestan in the battle of the Talas in the year 751, which was favourable to the caliph's armies. Whilst a half-Turkish military governor, An Lu-shan, damped down a praetorian rebellion in China, Islamization began in Turkestan. On the other hand the Uigurs in the Tarim area adopted the Nestorian and Buddhist traditions of the former Indoeuropean settlers of this region. As a result of the gradual Islamization of what later became Turkestan, which at the same time led to a freeing of the still Persian region around Balkh from Iranian influences, there arose a split between the Turkish-Mongolian tribes. In the west purely Islamic Turkish tribes were formed, whilst the Eastern Mongolians, who favoured Buddhism and Nestorian Christianity, showed themselves open to many religious influences.

The conflicts with the Arabs had greatly weakened the Persians. And so it was possible for a former Turkish slave to take possession of Afghan Ghazni in the year 962. The kingdom of the Ghaznaese was the first Turkish state in the Islamic area to play a part in world history. Its rulers turned towards India and thus began there the Moghul epoch, which did not end until 1857, but which ninety years later found a new political expression in part of the Indian subcontinent, in the modern state of Pakistan.

And once again the 'womb of the nations' sent forth new races to attack the ancient civilized states: the heathen Avars turned to the west, then followed the Pechenegs, who in their turn drove out the Magyars who had already penetrated to southern Russia. And again and again Europe trembled before these races. It was the Tartars, a Mongolian race, who had finally travelled overland by way of Russia and in the thirteenth century were threatening Central Europe.

One of the many Tartar-Turanian races of the Mongols, the Khazars, had established a highly civilized state on the steppes of southern Russia. They adopted Judaism and wanted to build a second Israel with the dynamic of the Central Asian steppe land. Their Khans gave their own daughters to East Roman emperors as wives. Empress Theodora, wife of Justinian II, and Empress Irene, wife of Constantine V, were born at the courts of the Khazars. The son of the latter, who defeated the Arabs in 778 at Germanicaeia, was called Leo the Khazar. The relationships between Khazars and Byzantines show that Turkish-Mongolian politics of the court of Byzantium still provide a splendid subject for research. The Khazars lived on in the Polish-Lithuanian region, as a small 'splinter' population, the Karamins, a unique race consisting of Jewish and Turkish elements—having its centres in Vilna, Halicz, Troki and Luck.

Seljuk and Osman Turks travelled along the overland routes across Anatolia to Europe. Yet they remained in Anatolia. When the 'golden apple' of the tree of their desire, Constantinople, fell— the Turkish races called their military and political aims *Kizil Elma*—the dynamic of the peoples of the steppes from the regions to the north and south of the Himalayas, blended with the civil tradition of Byzantium embracing church and empire, to form the modern kingdom of the Turkish sultans and caliphs. The second Rome on the Bosphorus had fallen. Two hundred years later the

most far-reaching attack of the Turks against Europe collapsed
before Vienna. The third Rome on the Moskva paid its willing
tribute to the Tartar kinsmen of the Turks, the lords of the
'Golden Horde'.

Before that point was reached Genghis Khan (Temüdchin is
his Mongolian name) was to forge a new Mongolian kingdom
urged to expansion by the dynamism of his troops of horsemen.
He won for himself the leadership of his race and of related tribes,
and welded all subject races so as to add the North Chinese and
North Iranian areas to Turkish Mongolian territory. His successors carried the offensive to Cambodia, Annam and Korea, and
even ventured, albeit in vain, to sea in order to attack Japan and
Java. Persia fell into the hands of the Ilkhans, descendants of
Jaghatai, the second son of Genghis Khan. Abaga, the son of
Hülagü, the conqueror of Persia, married Mary, the daughter of
the Byzantine emperor, Michael Palaeologue. He was the closest
friend of the Nestorian patriarchs Mar Denka and Jaballaha. In
the years 1274 to 1276 he sought contact with France, England
and the Papal See. There was no outcome. But it should not be
forgotten that in 1241 Europe had trembled before the selfsame
Mongolian race when Polish and German armies were together
destroyed on the battlefield of Wahlstatt, near Liegnitz, and that
shortly afterwards the Hungarians were so badly beaten on the
Sajó that their king hastily fled to Croatia. In addition Byzantium,
which had been subject to the Latin emperors from 1204 to 1261,
had just shaken off their yoke. Mutual mistrust prevailed in Constantinople, Rome, Paris, London and especially in Palermo,
where the conqueror of the Staufen, Charles of Anjou, was at
this very time preoccupied with the idea of overthrowing the East
Roman empire of Michael VIII (Palaeologue), newly established
after the destruction of Latin rule in Byzantine territory. Thus the
alliance promoted by a Byzantine princess, wife of a Mongolian
Khan, between the Christian thrones of Europe and Kurultai, the
seat of government in Karakorum in Mongolia, came to nothing.
But the stories of Nestorian Christians who ministered to the
Mongolians wove the medieval wreath of legends around the
kingdom of Prester John. The part played by Christianity amongst
the Mongolians is still emphasized in legend. In Peking, which was
called Khanbalik when it was the Mongolian capital, the Nestorian
patriarch of Bagdad was allowed to found an archbishopric as

early as 1275. And in 1289 a ministry for Christian affairs was set up in the Chinese Mongolian residency. Nevertheless the fact that scarcely fifty years after the Mongolian battle of Liegnitz a Franciscan monk, John of Montecorvino, was sent by Pope Nicholas IV to Peking, reveals a most realistic attitude on the part of the medieval Christians towards the Mongolians. After some twenty years' residence in China the same Franciscan monk became the first Latin archbishop of Peking, in the year 1307.

Whilst the Mongolian 'Golden Horde' ruled Russia and the 'White Horde' ruled Siberia, a Turk called Timur, born near Samarkand, seized power in the territory of Turkestan after a battle with the descendants of Genghis Khan, and named himself the re-founder of the Turkish-Mongolian empire. From his home-land he attacked the 'Golden Horde' in southern Russia, the Osmans, Iran and Bagdad also. All in the name of the Koran! Timur was a Mohammedan, but with all the reservations of the Mongolian Turk. His fanaticism and cruelty could not hold the countries he had overrun. The followers of Timur found them-selves obliged to give up their hereditary lands in Bokhara, which the Uzbeks were invading. In 1525 the Timurite Baber was com-pelled to retreat with his followers to Afghanistan. From there he pushed on to the Punjab and conquered Delhi. Thereupon the heirs of Timur began to prosper on new soil. Humayan and Akbar were the next great rulers of a dynasty which as Great Moghuls lent new splendour to the Mongolian name on Indian soil.

The Mongolians themselves retired from world history. At about that time in their native land the medieval tactical advantages of armies of horsemen had to yield to the Western development of firearms. At the right moment they prescribed for themselves an unwarlike religion. In 1577 Altan Khan proclaimed Tibetan Lamaism to be the Mongolian state religion. The Mongolians thereby began a new kind of relationship, namely a religious one, which linked them closely with the Tibetans.

The inhabitants of Tibet do not make an appearance in history until late in the seventh century A.D., with King Sron bTsan sgam po. His people were, like the Mongolians, a powerful race of warriors, who struggled successfully against the Nepalese and Chinese and played a leading part in Central Asia for about two hundred years. The Tibetan kings were skilled diplomats and formed lively relations even with the Arabs. Nevertheless, after the fourteenth century, when the monkish dynasties of the lamas, and later especially that of the Dalai Lama, had transformed the Buddhism of the country more and more into a religion of magic ritualism in which mere recitation was supposed to provide a road to salvation, the Tibetans retired as a political force from the stage of world affairs. Those who had been active under the kings became passive under the lamas, the pawns of neighbouring and distant powers.

In 1498 Portuguese ships reached the coast of Indian Malabar. Europeans had covered the sea route to India for the first time. The continental era of Asia, when the middle of the world was the axis of events, was over. The maritime, oceanic age was beginning. At the same time a spiritual contact between Europe and Asia was proclaimed. After the navigators came Christian missionaries. But just where the Portuguese had landed, Kerala, there had always been an ancient Christianity, living communities whose tradition went back to St Thomas, one of Christ's apostles. These Christians cannot be simply considered apart from the life of southern India, whilst history passed over the once flourishing Nestorian communities to the north of the Himalayas—just as the syncretic branch of Christianity, Manichaeism, also disappeared. In Kerala the Jewish communities, later divided into 'black' and 'white', also have a tradition as ancient as that of the Christians.

After the Portuguese, the oceanic epoch of the modern era brought English, Dutch, Danes and French to the shores of India, which became an intermediate station on the European route to the Far East.

A brief spell of dynamic energy on the part of the Burmese at the end of the eighteenth and especially at the beginning of the nineteenth century, when Assam fell into other hands, brought them into conflict with the East India Company. The Thai races, who penetrated for the first time in history, between the eighth and thirteenth centuries, from the Himalayan foothills of Yunnan into lower India, were the only peoples in this area who could defend themselves against the colonialist attack. As brief as the Burmese expansionist dream was that of the Persians in the eighteenth century, when Nadir Shah's troops marched as far as Delhi, and brought the Great Moghul's proudest symbol, the peacock throne, to Teheran. Even the might of the Afghans, who descended shortly after the Persian troops into the valleys of the Indus, could not in the long run change the map of the western half of India. However, this brave mountain race knew how to preserve their own freedom.

In the meantime tsarist Russia pressed slowly forward to the Himalayas. Her expansionist urge was halted on the Pamir ('roof of the world'). The heirs of the tsars are the Soviets. Japan confronted them as protagonists of a Greater Asia. In the Second World War Japanese soldiers stood ready in Manipur to march to Calcutta and Delhi. In the papers in their knapsacks one could read that they were setting out to place the home of the Buddha under the protection of the Tenno. Just as the Japanese were about to strike their greatest opponent in the Far East from the rear, where convoys travelled the Himalayan routes to Chungking and China, it was a new weapon which abruptly shattered their so-called dream kingdom, 'The Greater East Asian sphere of prosperity', for the morosely fighting Tenno soldiers—the first atom bomb fell. With the splitting of the nucleus the new age brought not only physical and finally military problems, but also set in motion a chain reaction of political and human questions. While discussion about the good or evil of this new thing was beginning, the Communist subcontinent of China was being formed.

The immense states of China, India and the Soviet Union are today gazing towards the continent, and between them arch the mountains which even today are peopled with gods by lamaistic Buddhists and pious Hindus. There is one common element in the history of these states: the recollection of the rigid organization which the Mongolian peoples of the steppes once imposed upon each one of these great empires.

History is a strange thing. We stand at the roadside and reflect upon what is happening. Around the Himalayas, peoples and races have often given dynamic expression to their longing. Today this longing is expressed in states which are the most populous upon earth. In the era now beginning, when the Western conception of an *élite* is slowly fading before the loud clamour of the age of the masses, that fact will give to this area its singular prevalence over other regions of the world.

In addition to the pilgrims, who were again and again liquidated by military conquerors, there came a new generation of Himalayan

c

explorers. The mountaineers of Europe and America were drawn to the mountains of the gods. With perseverance and courage they attacked the highest peaks, and, more so than the Alps, the Himalayas were destined to become the most daring goal of Western mountaineers.

Even if Alpinism names Petrarch as the first mountaineer known to us (at the beginning of the fourteenth century he climbed Mont Ventaux near Avignon just for fun), yet the modern type of mountain pioneer was not evolved until the nineteenth century. That was when, at the beginning of the century, the Genevan scholar Saussure, a friend of Goethe, offered a prize for the first ascent of Mont Blanc—and won the prize himself.

As the Swiss Saussure was the father of Alpinism, so the Englishman W. W. Graham for the first time, in 1883, turned the gaze of European mountain-lovers towards the Himalayas. He climbed many mountains, but his lack of geographical knowledge tricked him. The mountains which he claimed to have conquered could hardly have been climbed by him, because he confused the names. This still happened right into the twentieth century to explorers equipped with modern aids. Nevertheless to Graham belongs the credit of having discovered the Himalayas for mountaineering expeditions.

In 1892 the Englishman W. M. Conway led the first expedition to the region of the Karakorum. His companions were children of the Alps: Matthias Zurbriggen, who since his youth had felt the fascination of the highest peaks on the earth, and had been the first to climb the mightiest mountain of South America, Aconcagua, and O. Eckenstein, who as an authority on glaciers was able to compare the laws of the Himalayas with those of the other mountain ranges of the earth.

The Himalayan expeditions are moving stories, linked with individual mountains and ever binding the boldest with their spell. Above all other peaks Mount Everest shines majestically. At one time the highest point on earth was simply recorded as No. XV in the reports of the 'Survey of India' of the Indian Ordnance Office. It had been impossible to trace a native name. Thus in 1865 the mountain was named after a worthy ex-Director of the Ordnance Survey, the Surveyor-General George Everest. Later they discovered the name which the mountain peoples gave it: *Chonio Lungha*, which means something like 'Divine Mother of the Land'. Yet for the rest of the world the highest of all peaks in the mountains of the gods bears simply the name of an official of the former British government of India.

Ever since 1921, when the first British expedition with Colonel C. K. Howard-Bury set out to explore Mount Everest, the king of mountains had become the prerogative of the British. At that time George Mallory was amongst those who had completely devoted themselves to the unknown. From his Welsh home he brought to the Himalayas a word which signifies a high valley, and is written *cwm* ('combe' in English).

The Mount Everest expedition was continued from 1922 to 1924. Mallory, who had become the personification of the British mountaineering spirit, did not return. Again, in 1934, 1935, 1936, 1938, 1950 and 1951, the British attempted to storm the peak; in 1952 the Swiss began. A year later the mountain was conquered. The victors were the New Zealander Hillary and the Nepalese Sherpa Tensing. In June 1953, on the very day of her coronation, they were able to announce to Queen Elizabeth II the victory of a Commonwealth expedition over the highest mountain on earth.

Since 1932 German expeditions were going to Nanga Parbat, on the extreme north-west fringe of the Himalayas. Here the first climber, the Englishman Mummery, had lost his life in 1895. Since that time Nanga Parbat was 'the murderous mountain' for the British; for the Germans it was to be the fateful mountain of Asia.

In 1934 there occurred in the heights of ice and snow the tragedy of the Willy Merkl expedition, when a pitiless mountain fate claimed the best men amongst the German mountaineers. In 1953 Hermann Buhl managed to vanquish the mountain.

As the Germans possess their mountain in the Himalayas, so in 1950 the Frenchmen Maurice Herzog and Louis Lachinal climbed the first 25,000-footer, Annapurna ('the Goddess Giving Nourishment'); in 1955 the Frenchmen Lionel Terray and Jean Conzy succeeded in climbing Makalu for the first time; in 1956 the Japanese, in the persons of Imanishi, Kato and Higeta, conquered Manashi; likewise the Swiss climbers Reiss and Luchsinger triumphed over Lhotse, the Italians over Chogori (Great Mountain, also called K2 for short) in the Karakorum, where the victorious climb of 1954 belongs to Achille Campagnoni and Lino Lacedelli.

Nanga Parbat had often seen Austro-German expeditions. In

some mountains Austrian expeditions alone, or single climbers, had tried their hand. This was the case with Cho-Oyu, which Herbert Tichy and Sepp Jöchler climbed. The same is true of the mountains of Karakorum in the Baltovo territory such as Gasherbrum II (climbed in 1956 by Fritz Moravec, Sepp Larch and Hans Willenport) and Broad Peak (conquered in 1957 by Fritz Wintersteller, Kurt Diemberger, Markus Schmuck and Hermann Buhl). The exploratory attempt of Heinz Kruperz in 1953 declared Gosainthan, in southern Tibet, to be another Austrian goal.

Around Dhaulagiri (The White Mountain) a sporting contest has been going on for a long time among French, Germans, Swiss and Argentines. International expeditions have for some time been attempting two Himalayan peaks without success: for the first time in 1930, when an attack was made on *Kanch*, Kanchenjunga ('Five Sacred Caskets of the Great Snow'), on the frontier between Sikkim and Nepal, and in 1934, when Hidden Peak (or Gasherbrum I) in Karakorum was attempted.

In 1950 the Norwegians wrote their names in the 'visitors' book of the Himalayas'. Per Kvernberg then reached the top of Tirich Mir in Hindukush. In 1928 a Russo-German expedition with Alwein, Schneider and Wien had climbed Lenin Peak (Kauffmann Peak). Abalkor reached the top of Stalin Peak in 1933. In 1939 the Poles attempted the eastern summit of Tirsuli. Their failure was inevitable, as two of the expedition's porters had been engulfed by a fall of ice.

For some years the Chinese have been working on various Trans-Himalayan peaks. Similarly mountaineering is now becoming popular amongst young Indians. The Himalaya Institute in Darjeeling is the centre of these endeavours. But above all one should not forget the sons of the Himalayas, without whom scarcely one of the foreign mountaineers would have succeeded in pushing forward into the world of eternal ice. Sherpa Tensing must always be linked with Hillary, Sherpa Gyalzen with the Japanese conquerors of Manaslu. In 1934, when the German mountaineers set off on Nanga Parbat, they were accompanied on their fateful journey by men from the Hunsa and Balti region: Nima Dorje, Nima Tashi, Pintso Nurbu.

The Himalayas have created an international of sport such as no other mountain range on earth has formed, and they have today inspired the foundation of Himalayan societies from Tokyo to London. The German Himalaya foundation was formed in 1934 after the tragedy of Nanga Parbat became known.

Next to the conquerors who devoted themselves to the merciless struggle for the highest peaks, the names of the explorers and travellers in the Himalayas must be mentioned. In the fourth century, when the focal point of Europe was the basin of the Mediterranean, Fa Hsien took leave of China to seek the Indian land of Buddha. Sung Yung, and more especially Hsuan-chuang (Hsiung Tsiang), followed centuries later. They wanted to see the home of those Indians who had once brought them the gospel of Buddha such as Dharma-raksha (in Chinese Tamo-losa), Buddha-bhadra (in Chinese Chu Shien) and Jina-bhadra (in Chinese Chen Ti).

European interest in the Central Asian area began with the Flemish Franciscan monk William van Rysbroek and the Italians Giovanni Plano de Carpini and Marco Polo in the thirteenth century. The line descends from them to Johann Gruber in the seventeenth century, Father Desiderius in the eighteenth century, and the great researchers of the nineteenth and twentieth centuries —the generation of the brothers Schlagintweit, of Prjevalsky, De Filippi, Csoma de Körös, Dutreuil de Rhins, Sven Hedin and Wilhelm Filchner.

Many, many others came and made scientific investigations in the Himalayan region. But above all, the southern slopes of the Himalayas became the home of schools in which for a century the young generation of Indians had been educated in accordance with modern view-points. In the Indian part of the mountain ranges, where the spiritual kingdoms of Hindus, Buddhists, Confucians, Moslems and Christians clash, the British had at one time built row upon row of hill stations. And in them were the many Christian senior schools and colleges, soon followed by educational establishments of the Hindus, Moslems and Sikhs. These schools had one thing in common: a wish to educate young people to a belief in the Divine. If one looks at a map on which India's schools are marked, one has a momentary impression that a line of fortresses is drawn parallel to the frontier. And is it not that, this row of schools pressing closely upon each other, in the favourable climate of the frontier zone in the foothills of the Himalayas? Frontier defences of the spirit, where science and faith meet!

3

Tibetan Legend

THE MAGIC WORD IS DALAI LAMA

THE word 'Tibet' breathes mystery and magic for most Westerners, yet for many it is also only a vague geographical conception. But Tibet moved into the bright light of the present when insistent forces in the Indian continent and later in China brought about a reorganization of their states. Then Tibet too was caught up by the tide of political reorientation.

For Tibetans themselves, their country, where Kailas, the mountain of the world, lies, is the centre of the earth and the earthly reflection of the all-embracing cosmos. Tibet is the 'navel of the earth', as the Tibetans call it, *Ssa ji lTa ba*. Between the glaciers of the Himalayas in the south, and the steppes and inhospitable desert lands of the north, stretches the high plateau, into which the great river valleys are carved: those valleys that form green oases in summer and have become the homes of most of the population. The great rivers of eastern and southern Asia flow from the land of Tibet or have their source in the border territory of this 'navel of the earth'. From the Indus to the Brahmaputra, from the Irawadi, Salween, Mekong and Yang-tse Kiang to the Hwang-ho, the springs of Tibet or of the Sino-Tibetan frontier zone water the soil of the Indian, Indochinese and Chinese countryside.

Thus Tibet, with a present population of three or four millions, about a third of whose men live as lamas in the many monasteries of the country, has in past centuries almost always lived on the edge of events. The world of its people was different from that of

neighbouring races. Therefore the neighbours were moulders of
Tibet's fate to a greater extent than her own sons were.

The core of Tibet is in the eastern part, in the Yarlung region
to the south of the Brahmaputra, from which region, in the
seventh century A.D., the first historical character of this Central
Asian area made himself the sole ruler of the whole of Tibet. This
was Sron bTsan sgam po. His battles with Nepal and China were
so successful that he was able to begin a great game of world
politics and make an alliance with the Arabs. In about 715 the two
allies, Tibet and Arabia, even jointly established a king in Iranian
Ferghana, who served as a link between the Tibetan king and the
Arab caliphs.

But Harun al Rashid, the most popular of all the Abbassid
caliphs in Bagdad, looked to the West rather than to the East, and
neglected the Tibetan alliance. Militarily, of course, he relied upon
Iranian troops from Khorasan and Ferghana in modern Turkestan.
The uncertainty of aim as between military and political goals
hastened the dissolution of the Arabian empire. In Morocco the
Idrisids made themselves independent, as did the Aghlawids in
Tunisian Kairwan. At the same time Charlemagne sent an embassy
from Aix-la-Chapelle to Bagdad.

The western part of Islam, which received political preference
from Bagdad, showed its gratitude for this preference by political
decay. The eastern part—Khorasan—although it still took the lead,
especially in military matters, replied in a military manner by a
revolt which Harun himself had to set out to quell. He died on this
punitive expedition in the town of Tus. The Tibetan flank, where
the neglected former allies of the Arabians were passively watching
the rebellion in Khorasan, was exposed, and therefore the question
of Turkestan could not be decided. Then Harun's successor, Al-
Maimun, remembered the Tibetans and asked for renewal of
all the treaties. That was in 810. But in 822 a 'Stele'
was erected, which still stands in the Potala palace and on
which the first Sino-Tibetan treaty was chiselled. The monolith
informs us:

The Lord of Tibet, the divine King, full of wonderful strength, and
the great King of China, Hwang Te, nephew and uncle on the maternal
side, have agreed to unite their kingdoms. This great agreement was
made that it may always be faithfully kept and never changed. All gods
and men were called upon to be witnesses of the sacred oath. That this

may always be so from generation to generation, the terms of our alliance have been cut here in stone.

The King of wonderful strength, Ti-de-Tsen, and the Chinese King Bun Pu He-u Tig Hwang Te, nephew and uncle, united their kingdoms, confident that it would further the mutual well-being of Tibet and China, and that all men would receive much happiness, within and without, and that each and every one would be happy and prosperous for a long time.

Thus runs the old treaty, but it cannot be concealed that it was always difficult for the Chinese to rule in Tibet because the population took every opportunity of withdrawing from Chinese control.

Tibet remained a part of the East Asian world, and the unique opportunity of playing a part in world politics could not be used. In the place of external successes, internal inconsistencies suddenly made themselves felt. Through them the Tibetans experienced religious wars for the first time. Missionaries of Buddhism had crossed the Himalayas again and again, but King gLan dar Mar persecuted them between 836 and 842 by all possible means. To this end he favoured the *Bon* faith. This was a religion strongly permeated with magic and Shamanism. Bon priests have the reputation of being powerful magicians. They are said to conjure up demons, to rule over nature—especially hail—to heal the sick, and to be able to make astrological forecasts. The *Bon-po*—the adherents of the Bon religion—often make inquiries into the fate of their relations in the other world through these priest-magicians, by sending them on a 'reconnaissance after souls'. To do this the priests, clothed in blue and black garments, like the Shamans of eastern Siberia, go into a state of trance. Today much of the Christian inheritance lies dormant in the Bon religion. Manichaeans and Nestorians have greatly changed its character, which was originally purely Shamanistic. Buddhism brought about something else, after the discussions throughout the centuries ended in the adoption of some doctrines from Buddha's teaching. The Bon are still partly represented in Tibet proper, but they have the largest number of adherents in the Tibetan provinces of the North and South which were not under the jurisdiction of the Dalai Lama. A German research worker, Matthias Hermanns, even believed that the very heart of Tibetan nationhood lay in one of these Tibetan frontier lands. In his work, *The Nomads of Tibet*, he writes of the Amdo, who are known elsewhere in European literature as Tunguts and dwell in the Koko Nor province, that they are the actual bearers of *Bod yul*, the land of Bod, as the Tibetans call their home. Hermanns rejects the view that this Bod signifies Buddha. According to him, Bod is the tribal ancestor of this race.

However, Buddhism became known in the capital at the time of the first Tibetan king. Sron bTsan sgam po had two wives, princesses from China and Nepal. But in the times which followed there were again and again difficulties for the teaching of Buddha. It is true that in the tenth and eleventh centuries an intensified missionary drive established his doctrine in the minds of the people, but it soon led to dissensions. The reformer Tson K'a pa (1357–1419) called forth a great movement towards unity. He came from the region of the aforementioned Amdo Tibetans, and wanted to give priority above other sects to his own lamaistic interpretation of Buddha's teaching, in a Tibet which in the course of the centuries had become completely Buddhist—apart from the few remaining Bon. Ever since this time only two sects have actually played a part amongst the Tibetans: the sect called Tson K'a po of the 'Yellow Ones'—or *dge Lugspa*, which means 'virtuous sect' —and that of the 'Red Ones', whose significance is fading steadily. The 'Yellow Ones' are predominant, and the great lamas who attained world fame belong to this sect. The successors of the first pupil of Tson K'a pa since about 1470 have been held to be the incarnation of Bodhisattva Avalokitesvara. *Bodhisattva* is a person who has been called to highest perfection, that is to say, somebody who is close to attainment of Buddha-dom, but renounces it out of pity for other creatures and in order to smooth their road to perfection. Whilst the Dalai Lama is considered to be the earthly embodiment of the Bodhisattva Avalokitesvara, the other high lama of Tibet, the Panchen Lama, is held to be image of Buddha Amitibha.

In the thirteenth century, after the proclamation of the Mongolian Qubilai (Kubla Khan) as Great Khan and simultaneously as Emperor of the Chinese, Tibet became politically part of Mongolian China, whose dynasty took the name Yuan. In past centuries the Chinese emperors had only now and then entered into brief political relationships with Tibet, which, in spite of vows of eternal loyalty, can count only as interludes.

Following the union with the Mongolian rulers of China, there began the dependence upon the 'Middle Kingdom', which was stressed again and again from the Chinese side, but which was generally only nominal. The Mongolians who, soon after the death of Genghis Khan, had come under the influence of Buddhism, ruled mildly in Tibet in the subsequent years. There came about a kind of community of fate between Tibetans and Mongolians, especially after the sons of Genghis Khan bowed before Buddha and his teaching, and honoured as their spiritual leader the Grand Lama of Tibet, who was a follower of Tson K'a pa.

The first pupil of this reformer, Ganden-Truppa (1391–1474) is reckoned as the first in the succession of the Grand Lamas who later received the name of Dalai Lama (that is, 'Ocean-wide Lama'), that magic word which was later to fascinate Western men so greatly.

It was the third Grand Lama, Sonam Gyatso, who in 1580 went to Mongolia, where Lamaism had been accepted as the official religion for three years, in order to direct the fate of his communities for eight years from there. When he died Tibetan-Mongolian relationships were deepened still further, because his rebirth was discovered in the Mongolian royal family. This fourth Grand Lama, bSod-nam-srgyam-tso, was the first to bear officially the name of Dalai Lama, a designation in which a Mongolian word was combined with a Tibetan one, thus announcing the future spiritual community of Mongolians and Tibetans. The Mongolian fourth Dalai Lama gave a special gift to his countrymen: in 1602 he confirmed a Mongolian reincarnation of another *Bodhisattva* near Urga: Maidari Khutuktu.

When in 1924 the last in the succession of these three greatest Buddhist incarnations, Je-tsün tam-pa, died as head of state in Outer Mongolia, which had meanwhile become Communist, the reincarnation was no longer continued, because it did not please the Soviet Russians.

The sovereignty of China, which Tibet had always felt to be nominal, was forgotten for a time when the Manchus ascended the imperial throne of Peking. However, the Manchus did not forget Tibet. They invited the fifth Dalai Lama to Peking, where an unwritten concordat controlled their relations from that time onwards: the Chinese governed Tibet and respected the Dalai Lama as politically highest amongst the lamas, but he was allowed to speak only as a spiritual authority. It is curious that the Panchen Lama (or Tashi Lama) yielded place more and more to the Dalai Lama, although the former was intended to be a 'higher embodiment' and actually also higher ranking. The political situation in Tibet remained unchanged. The Dalai Lamas continued to summon the faithful to worship by means of mussel shells, as they had done for centuries—the sixth, it is true, also found time to write really profane love songs, which are still sung today by young Tibetans—and, seen from Peking, their country was nothing but an inhospitable land. It was a kind of punishment to be sent there as a Chinese official.

Tibet did not gain political importance again until the European powers—Russia and England—appeared on the scene. The British first took an interest in Tibet in 1768, when the Court of Directors of the East India Company decided to seek out possibilities of trading in the land of the Dalai Lama and in western China. However, no economic or political relations developed between India and Tibet until the Gurkhas of Nepal were suddenly involved in a war with the Chinese. At this juncture the Nepalese quickly made a commercial treaty with the British, although until then they had adopted a very hostile attitude towards them. During the war between Nepal and China, Lord Cornwallis, the Governor-General of Calcutta, received a letter from the Chinese commander-in-chief, Marshal Fu-K'ang-an, dated 31st March 1792, asking for the support of the British against the Nepalese troops. Similarly the Dalai Lama and the Panchen Lama wrote to him, the former in Tibetan, the latter in Persian. In spite of these beginnings of diplomatic correspondence, Tibet remained closed, even though individual Britons attempted to cross the Himalayas, as, for example, Thomas Manning, who in 1811 was the first Englishman to reach the court of Lhasa.

Tibet had as a matter of fact been the goal of other Europeans for long enough, and here it was especially a question of Christian missionaries. The Jesuits tried often enough to penetrate into Tibet from India. In the years between 1603 and 1607 Benedict Goes undertook a dangerous journey from Agra, which in fact took him more to the north, to Khotan and Turfan. Desiderius visited Tibet between 1714 and 1722. At the same time the Italian Capucins had begun their Tibetan mission (1713). From 1625 to 1640 there was already a Christian mission to Tibet in Tsaparang, which today is unfortunately almost forgotten. At that time the ruler of Guge was about to be converted to Christianity in the mission founded by Father Andrade, but a war with Ladakh lost him the throne and his plan could not be carried out. The inhabitants of Guge, who had become Christians, were taken away as slaves. The vision of a Catholic Himalayan empire vanished.

In the Treaty of Nanking, concluded in 1842 between the British and Chinese, which opened five treaty ports to the British, there were no clauses providing for trade with Tibet. This situation lasted until 1876 when, in the Convention of Ch'i-fu (concluded on 13th September), England reserved the right to carry out negotiations for British trade missions in Tibet also. By the Convention of Ch'i-fu China established diplomatic foreign embassies, first in London, then in Berlin (1877), Paris, Washington, Tokyo (1878), St Petersburg and Madrid (1879).

In the past decades the British had striven to improve their position in Nepal, Sikkim and Bhutan, and, since the two latter in particular had long-standing connections with Tibet, they had at the same time to come to terms with this country. It was not until 17th March 1890, in an agreement signed in Calcutta by the Governor-General of India, Lord Lansdowne, and the Chinese governor in Lhasa, Sheng-t'ai, that the British succeeded in separating Sikkim politically from Tibet and placing it under British protection. The Tibetans showed no inclination to keep this convention. Their words to the British and Chinese were the same: 'We are not parties to the convention and do not feel ourselves bound.'

In recent years the Chinese themselves had suffered one reverse after another, in both diplomatic and military affairs: Korea, Annam and Burma had had to renounce their loyalty to Peking. At this favourable moment the British tried to start conversations with Lhasa, so as to gain for themselves influence and opportunities for trade in Tibet.

In this situation the shadow of Russia fell across Tibet. The warm relationship between Tibetans and Mongolians has already been mentioned. The Russians, who knew of this connection, secured Mongolian agents in order to gain influence over the Tibetans. It was the time when the thirteenth Dalai Lama played a skilful part in world politics. Of course the spiritual diplomat from the roof of the world was waging an unequal struggle. He had to deal with world powers, whilst the only recourse left to him was a skilful playing off of one great one against another.

In their treatment of the Mongolians, the Russians always showed good psychological insight. After the long-standing remembrance, mingled with fear and terror, of the Mongolian-Tartar period of their history, there came in the nineteenth century an intellectual literary reaction, in which a new interpretation of their relationship to the Mongolians began. The Russians rediscovered amongst the Mongolians the dynamic strength, the action, which is necessary if a fresh wind is to blow through the landscape of ageing civilizations. It was the period when Russia felt an aversion from Europe and a corresponding inclination towards Asia. It was at one and the same time the intellectual under-pinning and the justification of the tsarist Asian policy, carried forward more and more ruthlessly.

In his *Dnevnik pisatelya* (the 'Diary of a Writer'), Dostoyevsky had already challenged the Russians to take up a positive attitude towards Asia. 'We must free ourselves from the slavish fear of being called "Asiatic barbarians", more Asian than European, by Europe.'

The Orthodox religious philosopher, N. F. Fyodorov, looked to the Himalayas, to Pamir, and challenged the Tsar to assume the title 'Pamirski', in order to indicate that the area where lay the grave of the first man, Adam, had come under the protection of Russia. It was Russia's task to be the guardian of this grave, and also of that of the second Adam, Christ—in the latter case in succession to the Emperor of the Second Rome.

From these heralds of Asia, the intellectual path of the Russians turned towards Asia and passed by way of the Pan-Mongolianism of Solovyev, who out of his Christian chiliastic longing greets the rise of Asia as the end of history, to Alexander Blok, who amidst the turmoil of the revolution announced his 'Scythian Ideas' in verse:

'. . . Yes, Scythians, we are Asiatics!
We gaze greedily out of our slit-shaped eyes . . .'

And so it is no wonder that amongst the lamaistic Buryat and Kalmuck subjects of the Tsar, some regarded Russia as their fate. These Asiatic Mongolian friends of Russia identified the great future kingdom of eternity, Shambhala, the land of the North, with the state of the tsars.

In 1893 a memorandum by the politically interested Doctor
Badmaiev was laid upon Alexander III's desk in which he indicated that lamaistic ideas must be given more attention in Russia.
That was a prerequisite of an increase in the power of the Tsar
over these regions. The lamas desired it. Tibet must be the immediate goal of Russian endeavours. In order to attain a successful
Asian policy, Russia should now train diplomats who were not
influenced by Europe. Under the thirteenth Dalai Lama, Ngag-
dbang Lo-bzang Thub-Idan, an experienced Buryat-Mongolian
played an important part. He was Agran Doryiyev, whose Tibetan
name was Nag-dban-rDo-rJe. Twice, in October 1900 and July
1901, the latter was sent by the spiritual and political leader of
Tibet to St Petersburg, where he was received in audience by the
Tsar Nicholas II. At the second visit he was able to present himself as Ambassador Extraordinary of Tibet. Doryiyev made to the
ruler of all the Russians a proposition no less than that he should
declare himself the protector of Buddhism and should see it as
Russia's task to be a liberator of the Asiatic peoples.

It is understandable that the appearance of Doryiyev on the
Neva quickly put Great Britain on the alert. A month after the
last audience of Doryiyev, in August 1901, the British Foreign
Minister, Lord Lansdowne, instructed his ambassador in St
Petersburg to inform the Russian Foreign Minister, Count
Lamsdorf, that the Government of His Britannic Majesty
would not remain indifferent if an attempt was made from any
direction to change the present status of Tibet. Another empire's
attention was roused: the State of the Tenno. And it is remarkable
that in the same year both island states set about defending themselves against the continental power of Russia. Japan saw the
Tsar's influence growing fatefully in that area which she claimed
as her sphere of interest in the Far East. But Great Britain wanted
to steal a march upon Russia, so as to remove Tibet from tsarist
influence.

Therefore in the year 1904 a British expeditionary force under
Younghusband marched to Lhasa in order to open the trade route
from India to China. A convention with the Tibetans gave the
British the right to set up three trading stations on Tibetan soil:
Gyantse, Gartok and Yatung. The convention was extended in
1906 to China, who then accepted the conditions. However, in
1910 the Manchu emperors sent troops into the country to

reinforce their rule over the land of the Dalai Lama. The spiritual lord of the Potala palace fled to Darjeeling. Meanwhile the Chinese emphasized that Nepal and Bhutan were vassal states of China and Tibet. It is true that a treaty between England and Bhutan had helped to hinder this development, but Chinese disturbances intervened. They were the starting signal for the first great October Revolution of modern times, when, on the tenth day of the tenth month in the year 1911, the Middle Kingdom lost its imperial and monarchic character and became a republic.

Whilst the Manchu emperors were being obliged to yield to the republican revolutionaries, the Dalai Lama proclaimed the independence of Tibet, which lasted from 1911 to 1949. In 1912 Tibet issued the first postage stamps. The stamps which appeared until 1950 are not exactly beautiful, to be sure, but they are nevertheless small paper witnesses of a modern expression of the sovereignty which before 1911 was just Chinese suzerainty, an iridescent word for the status of a country which, internally autonomous, has handed over its foreign policy to the government of another state. There has been no lack of Chinese attempts to change circumstances in Tibet once more; since about 1933, after the death of the thirteenth Dalai Lama, there have been some Tibetans who tried of their own accord to find means of reunion with China. But the majority was against it, and therefore the regent Ra-dreng Hutukhtu, abbot of the Ra-dreng monastery, who was friendly to China, came to grief. Yet there was no more good fortune in the choice of his successor, who drew up a rigorous system of government. In the course of the internal struggles and intrigues, the Panchen Lama went to China, and when he died his reincarnation soon came likewise under Chinese influence.

When the Communist government of Mao Tse-tung was proclaimed in 1949, the claim to Tibet was immediately re-established. India was interested at once, and the developments in the neighbouring country were closely observed. On 25th October 1950 the troops of Red China moved into Tibet; on 26th October 1950 they occupied Lhasa. The 'agreement on measures for the peaceful liberation of Tibet' was signed on 23rd May 1951 in Peking. The Dalai Lama had in fact appealed to international public opinion, but protests were of no avail. The Austrian Heinrich Harrer lived in Tibet for seven years before the Communist entry and was witness of the events which took place on the 'roof of the world' shortly before the *Anschluss*. He reported on these events in detail in his book *Seven Years in Tibet*.

The Dalai Lama's protest against the entry of Red China into his country had been unavailing. He soon returned home from his brief flight from the soldiers of Peking, stripped, it is true, of all political power. Those nearest to him advised a policy of 'Wait and see'. Today both Tibetan Grand Lamas are pretty, decorative pawns in Peking's Buddhist game, a wonderful opportunity of showing that Buddhism and Marxism are not incompatible. The Buddhist card is one of the many which are intermingled in the game of world politics in Tien An Men, the old imperial city in northern China.

The 'Case of Tibet', moreover, was to enrich the political 'double talk' of today by a treaty. In it the 'five principles' were formulated for the first time. This Tibetan Treaty, concluded between India and China on 29th April 1954, brought to an end the special status of the land of the Dalai Lama and recognized it as an autonomous region within the Chinese People's Republic. Thereby, for the first time, the following general principles were established, which were to regulate the relationship of the states with each other:

1. Mutual respect for the state of possession and sovereignty.
2. Disavowal of all acts of aggression.
3. Non-interference in the internal affairs of the other country.
4. Equality of rights and preservation of mutual advantages.
5. Peaceful co-existence.

In 1956, on the occasion of the two thousand five hundredth anniversary of the death of Buddha, the Dalai Lama and the Panchen Lama Ngoerhtehni visited India also. It was the first time that these two supreme dignitaries had made a state visit to a foreign country.

It is strange how far the two neighbouring countries of Tibet and India are removed from each other intellectually. What worlds divide the countries on both sides of the Himalayas! And how moved the spectator is during such a visit. A breath of far-off exotic distance touches us at the sound of the Dalai Lama's name. The institution of this priest-ruler over the people of Tibet is unique. He lives far away in the mysterious city of Lhasa, in the fairy-tale Potala palace, and myth and legend have helped to spread around him the magic of the unapproachable and divinely distant.

Then suddenly one is face to face with a laughing, black-spectacled young man who today embodies the tradition of the Dalai Lama. People of his race, living as merchants or shepherds anywhere along the southern slopes of the Himalayas, from Bhutan, Sikkim, Nepal or Ladakh in Kashmir, have travelled hundreds and hundreds of miles to do honour to the head of lamaistic Buddhism.

On 22nd December 1956 I was witness of a Buddhist tree ceremony. In the Buddha-Vihara in Mehrauli, outside the gates of Delhi, there stood a young shoot of the pipala or Bô-tree from Budh-Gaya. Once under the fig-tree of Budh-Gaya the monk Gautama, the 'enlightened one', had become the Buddha. Since that time Buddhists all over the world have tried to obtain a cutting from this tree which is sacred to them. Thus Asoka's son, who was already active as a Buddhist missionary, brought such a cutting to the royal city of Ceylon, Anuradhapura.

Because of the two thousand five hundredth anniversary of the entry of Buddha into Nirvana, the year 1956 saw in India one Buddhist celebration after another. Scholars from all over the world, whose field of research is Buddhism, had hastened to a Buddhist symposium, in order to pay their tribute in New Delhi to India's greatest son. This tribute was scientific in that an attempt was made to assess the intellectual position of Buddhism. Nothing is more difficult than that, for there can scarcely be a greater difference than there is between the Hinayana Buddhism of Ceylon and south-eastern Asia, and the Mahayana of the Far East. In between are the adherents of the lamaistic groups of the Himalayan countries and the Tibetan-Mongolian regions. Here magic has replaced the ethical discipline which was Buddha's aim.

For the first time an attempt was made in New Delhi to find a formula uniting all the adherents of Buddhism. But it was only a polite discussion over and around the matter. How could there be a unity between those people who on the one hand see in the Buddha absorption in the Absolute, a state of happiness without feeling and suffering, and those who on the other hand believe him to be ever born anew in one of the lamaistic leaders of Tibet? How is a magic formula of unity possible where on the one side cold reason denies almost everything metaphysical, whilst on the

D

other, the mere simple recitation of magic formulae and the primitive technique of a prayer mill are supposed to translate one to the region of metaphysics?

Nevertheless there remains a certain demonstration of pan-Buddhism running through this first all-Buddhist symposium on the soil of India, which has long ceased to be Buddhist. Mahatheras from Hinayana-Buddhism, that is to say, the heads of the Buddhist monasteries in Ceylon, Burma, Thailand and Cambodia, sat at the same table with lamas from Mongolia, Tibet and Sikkim and with Buddhist priests from Japan, China and Vietnam. The most impressive event was, however, the arrival of the Tibetan church leaders—the Dalai Lama and the Panchen Lama.

The Dalai Lama had been invited to India several times, but the answer was always: He cannot come. And then he was there. He climbed down from the roof of the world, accompanied by a staff of the highest officials, the so-called 'Lotus-footed ones'.

When one sees the smiling, youthful Dalai Lama, one is transferred to a primeval age of magic, when kings still walked upon the earth as the sons of god. The Panchen Lama always sits motionless; his smile gives the impression of a statue. One believes that Asia's mistrust lies hidden behind this frozen smile. But the Dalai Lama has lively eyes, glancing hither and thither. Sometimes one sees a roguish wrinkle in the corners of his eyes. Nevertheless one dreams of the age of magic. Suddenly a camera is drawn out. A flash-light flares up. It does not disturb the Panchen Lama. But the Dalai Lama (shall I meanwhile reveal his full name? He is called Geston Ngwang Lbsang Tengin Gyapso Sisunwanggyur Tschungpa Mapai Dhepal Sangpo—that is to say: 'the only holy one, the tender glory, powerful of word, pure in spirit, of divine wisdom, preserver of the faith, ocean-wide'), the Dalai Lama, the fourteenth of a long succession, has bent forward in a way quite unlike a Dalai Lama. He follows closely every movement of the amateur photographer. One sees that he would now like to leave his throne with its golden brocade canopy in order to ask with interest about the make, the price, black-and-white or colour films and suchlike, as all inquiring students do here.

As I was coming away from the short tree ceremony, one of the Sikkimese princes smiled at me. I asked him what was amusing him so much. Amusing him? Had I not felt that the sacred shadow of the Bô-tree, of the tree of illumination, had fallen upon me? It was as holy as the tree. Of course I could not feel this, poor sceptical son of distant Europe that I was. The holy tree seemed to me a tree like any other. And the Dalai Lama—a nice boy. That is my recollection of him.

It is of such scenes taken from the picturesque course of the now vanished Tibetan legend that one must inevitably think in order to escape from the terrifying spectacle now offered by the contemporary history of Tibet, for who now will venture to deny that a frightful conclusion is being attempted through the forced absorption of the Tibetan people into the Communist society of the People's Republic of China? The struggle in Tibet reached its height in the dramatic flight of the Dalai Lama to India in March 1959. Shortly after his arrival on Indian soil, a high Tibetan official announced from Tezpur in the North-Eastern Frontier Agency that he had fled from Tibet of his own free will. What the Chinese headquarters in Lhasa described as an 'invitation' to visit them constituted a danger of the Dalai Lama being held as a hostage in Communist hands or suffering some worse fate. The people in Lhasa knew very well that this sort of thing had gone on in Hungary in 1956, and they knew too how the will of the people was suppressed in 1953 both in East Berlin and in East Germany. Popular feeling was particularly roused in India by the flight of the Dalai Lama. The foreign observer in India was able to sense during those years how political feeling and popular influence ran in relation to foreign affairs. Such an attitude had never become noticeable since the rising in Hungary.

The Dalai Lama became ever more vocal about the tragic events in his home country, but he was forbidden to establish a government in exile in India. Nevertheless, contrary to the advice of the Indian Government, he determined to request the United Nations to mediate between China and Tibet. The brother of the High Lama, Gyalo Thondup, whom correspondents delighted to call 'foreign minister of the exiled Tibetan Government' (which was never formed), travelled to New York, and got the U.N.O. delegates of Ireland and Malaya to listen to him and bring the case of his people before the world forum. They proposed a debate which lasted for two days, and ended on 21st October in a resolution deploring the events in Tibet and calling for respect for the fundamental human rights of the Tibetan people.

For his part the Dalai Lama expounded the plight of his people in courageous and determined fashion from his successive places of refuge at Mussoorie and Dharamsala. On 7th August 1960 the International Commission of Jurists at Geneva had published a report running to 343 pages under the title *Tibet and the Chinese People's Republic*, in which this acknowledged aggression by the Chinese in Tibet was characterized as genocide, and further proved that Peking was trying to break down the social and religious structure of Tibet, that it had outraged most of the human rights formulated in U.N.O. declarations and that finally Tibet had been an independent state, *de facto*, previous to 1951. The Panchen Lama found himself forced to play a degrading part in the tragedy of Tibet by declaring, on 24th October 1960, that he condemned the inclusion of Tibetan affairs in the agenda of the United Nations Organization, since it interfered in the internal affairs of China. But still the misery of Tibet remains unrelieved, an immediate fact about a country that once seemed to us dim with the mists of legend.

In the meantime the battle for a 'progressive' development goes on in Tibet. The case of Tibet does not concern China alone. That is what the Chinese Tieh-Tseng Li expressed in his book, *The Historical Status of Tibet*, which appeared in 1956:

Whatever the world situation may be, the author believes that an understanding between India and China such as exists between the United States and Canada, with an agreement on the demilitarization of the Himalayas, which are the decisive element of both Indian and Chinese geography, offers not only a guarantee of the autonomous state of Tibet, but is also a stabilizing factor for world peace.

4

Medieval Epic

IN NEPAL, BHUTAN AND SIKKIM
TIME STANDS STILL

THE King of Nepal may be addressed five times with the title
Shri: 'Shri Shri Shri Shri Shri'. That is the highest form of
respect, for five is a sacred number. It is the due of the king, the
sole Hindu monarch still reigning, for he is a reincarnation of the
god Vishnu. Tibet is not far away with its reincarnations of
the lamas. But the living embodiment of Vishnu reminds us rather
of those Pharaohs in whom Amon-Râ, the supreme god of the
country of the Nile, was reborn. In Asia the present can even today
still be so far removed from us. And yet it is also close, for the
young king, Mahendra Bir Bikram Shah, wishes to lead his
country from the Middle Ages into the Modern Age. Therefore
he is honestly trying to introduce democratic reforms. This is by
no means easy, for not only are the methods of mountain cultivation in this clearly agricultural state those which we like to call
medieval, but also the mentality of the people belongs to the twelfth
rather than to the twentieth century.

The position of the kingdom of Nepal is of great geopolitical
significance, lying as a barrier between India and the territory of
the People's Republic of China, which claims Tibet as a part of
its territory. Just as the new Communist Government in Peking
was preparing to order its troops to the Himalayas, New Delhi
issued a declaration that the territory of Nepal belonged to the
Indian sphere of interest. This declaration showed the Chinese

43

how far they might go. It must not be forgotten that Nepal was formerly a Chinese vassal state, just as Bhutan and Sikkim as subordinate lands had been subject to Tibet. Just at this time an internal revolution broke out in Nepal.

Since the sixth century Nepal had seen numerous ruling houses, which across the valleys of the Himalayan foothills ruled over a race of peasants, breeders of cattle and collectors of berries. These were the Kiratsidi, the Lichchau, the Thakuri, the Malla and the Tirhut. When the Malla once again placed themselves in command in Nepal, they gave the country the most outstanding king who had ruled over them for centuries: Yakshamalla, who occupied the throne from 1426 to 1476. In 1767 the Gurkhas became rulers of Nepal. The first of the dynasty was Prithvi Narayan Shah, from the village of Gurkha, some four days' march from Katmandu, the capital of the country. Attacks from the Tibetan direction, from Kashmiri traders, the Gosains and finally from the British, were to be in store for the new ruling house. Yet Prithvi Narayan's successors knew how to build a solid state stretching from the eastern frontiers of Sikkim to the River Sutlej. A few years later the Nepalese Army, incited by the brother of the deceased Panchen Lama, Dza-Marpa, attacked Tibet. But in the two-year Sino-Nepalese war, which lasted from 1790 to 1792, the aggressors were defeated and had to accept hard terms. Nepal became a vassal state of the Middle Kingdom, like Korea, Annam, Siam and Burma. They were compelled to send a mission to Peking every five years to pay tribute. These terms were carried out until 1908. It was not until the Chinese revolution that the position was changed.

The Nepalese had scarcely forgotten the defeat of the Sino-Nepalese war when they attacked three police posts in Butwal, a contested area. That was in 1814; but the British Governor-General made a rapid decision and marched his troops into Nepal. He defeated the Nepalese, and on 2nd December 1815 dictated to them the Treaty of Sagauli, in which they were compelled to give up Sikkim and surrender the regions of Kumaon and Garhwal to the British. As a matter of fact it was a long time before the Nepalese accepted the treaty, but at the same time a change was taking place in the political life of the state.

In 1816, just as the war was ended, General Bhimsena Thapa seized power in the country without deposing the weak king, whose dynasty had suffered many losses in two wasteful wars. Bhimsena was in fact driven out in 1839, but a relation, Jung Bahadur, who, like the exiled lord of the country, came from the Rana family, managed to become hereditary prime minister with the title of Maharajah. The proud title of *Maharajah-dhiraj*'—'Almighty King'—was left for the nominal ruler. Thus there arose in Nepal a state system reminiscent of the Frankish Mayors of the Palace at the time of the Merovingians, or of the Japanese Shoguns. This rule of the Rana family as hereditary occupants of the post of prime minister ended on 18th February 1951. After various attempts by different politicians to form a government, the king, father of the present ruler, took the reins firmly in his hand. It was the policy of the Rana to allow no wind of change to blow into the country. On the other hand the young king endeavoured slowly to open all doors to the modern era with its political demands. To do this, not only is a gradual internal development necessary, but also contact with the outside world. Until the British withdrawal from India there had been since 1934 only one diplomatic representative in Nepal's capital Katmandu, namely, the British, and down to 1958 no one except India and Britain had diplomatic representation actually in Katmandu.

But after the proclamation of Indian independence an Indian Embassy was set up, and thereafter more and more diplomatic missions were added. While in 1958 only a few states had simultaneously accredited their representation also to the court of the King of Nepal—the U.S.A., Switzerland, the Soviet Union, France, the People's Republic of China, Japan, Burma and the Federal Republic of Germany—today there are some thirty countries having diplomatic relations with Nepal. Actually in the capital five powers maintain embassies, Britain, India, the U.S.A., the Soviet Union and China. The postal monopoly bequeathed by the British to the Indians was now transferred to the Nepalese. Nepal has for some time been a member of the World Postal Union, and the stamp catalogues of the world are already recording the history of its small and valuable stamps.

British-Nepalese relations began with a trade agreement made with the Gurkhas on 1st March 1792. But the motive was not so much a desire to carry on trade as the necessity caused by the Sino-Nepalese war. It was not until the Treaty of Sagauli that a close relationship was brought about between Nepalese and British.

The mountainous country was of the greatest importance for the rulers of India, because here the Gurkhas, the last true mercenaries in the world, were recruited for the Indian Army.

The Nepalese had often attempted by means of armed force to create for themselves a right of consultation in Tibetan affairs. In 1856 they therefore attacked Tibet once more, in order to establish a representative of their country in Lhasa and to protect Nepalese trade with Tibet. The warlike enterprise was successful, and in the same year on the 'eighteenth day of the second month in the year of the Fire Dragon' the Nepalese dictated a mild treaty to the Tibetans. The substance of the first three of the ten paragraphs was as follows:

1. The Tibetan Government shall pay each year to the Gurkha Government the sum of ten thousand rupees as a gift.
2. Gurkha (that is, Nepal) and Tibet have always shown respect to the Great Emperor. Tibet, as the country of monasteries, hermits and lamas, has dedicated itself completely to religion. For that reason the Gurkha Government declares itself prepared in the future to provide for Tibet, as far as possible, help and protection in case a foreign state should attack it.
3. In future Tibet will not demand any customs duty or road charge or taxes of any kind from the merchants or other subjects of the Gurkha Government.

For exactly one hundred years ten thousand rupees were collected every year in Lhasa for the royal treasury in Katmandu. The last 'gift' was delivered in 1956. After the visit to Peking of the Nepalese Premier of that time the treaty between Tibet and Nepal was so altered that 'terms degrading' to Tibet were struck out of it.

The pact of perpetual friendship with the British had been signed on 21st December 1923. In it Nepal's independence was recognized, but the word 'sovereignty' was not used. On 9th November 1947 an agreement had been reached between Great Britain, the Indian Union and Nepal upon the future of the Gurkha regiments in the Indian Army. In 1950 the status of the country changed, because for the first time the sovereignty of Nepal was attested in a diplomatic document. This was the pact of peace and friendship of 31st July 1950 between India and Nepal, which *inter alia* laid upon both parties the duty of 'recognizing and respecting the full sovereignty, territorial integrity and independence of each other'. On the same day a trade and economic treaty valid for ten years was signed between Katmandu and New Delhi.

The pact of peace and perpetual friendship with the British was renewed on 30th October 1950. The Government of Nepal announced on 14th July 1953 that the British Government was empowered for five years to recruit from Nepalese territory Gurkha soldiers for the British Army overseas.

Of the three Himalayan principalities, Nepal is by far the most open to new ideas. That is partly because of its status: it is a sovereign state. Conditions in the interior are as they were hundreds of years ago; but a small class is enlightened and seeks to gain for Nepal a stronger voice in the concert of the nations.

When therefore, in February 1958, at a Geneva conference of delegates from inland countries, the position of these states with regard to their access to the sea was discussed, Nepal became the spokesman of a group. This group wanted to have replaced by an international law the behaviour of the maritime nations towards the inland countries in questions of commerce, whereby they had been in the habit, until then, of allowing a certain international politeness to prevail.

Use was also made in Nepal of the possibility of improving the country's economy by means of loans. American, Indian and Chinese currency are to give help here. Nepal has been glad to be discovered by politicians bringing offers of help.

After the proclamation of King Tribhuvana on 18th February 1951 Nepal once more had a monarch willing to live up to his responsibilities. A romantic young German lady named Erika Leuchtag played her part in the royal drama of those days shortly before the fall of the Ranas, for she was the link between the hermetically imprisoned king and the Indian ambassador. There now began a miniature exercise in royal politics. After the death of the first Nepalese monarch of the post-Rana era, King Tribhuvana having died at Zürich in the year 1955, King Mahendra Bir Bikram took over the government. While the Ranas had persistently pursued a pro-British policy and had stood firm by Great Britain even at the time of the Mutiny in 1857, it seemed after the events of 1951 that the royal house of Nepal would insist on a strong pro-Indian line.

But international politics in the country had not yet crystallized.

The first Cabinet appointed by the king, of ten ministers, contained about half members of the Rana family, while the other half were drawn from the Nepalese Congress Party. But in November the Congress minister declared that such a Cabinet was not viable. Therefore, on 16th November 1951, a new Cabinet excluding the Ranas was formed. The last representatives of the old oligarchy therefore disappeared.

Development, however, was not steady, but frequently interrupted. Thus it came about that on 10th August 1952 the Prime Minister, Matrika Prasad Koirala, after severe criticism by his own brother, Bishewar Prasad Koirala, resigned from the sixty-one-strong Advisory Assembly, leaving the king to take over the administration personally. It was not until 15th June 1953 that a new Cabinet was appointed. The Prime Minister was the same Matrika Prasad Koirala as before, and again his own brother reproached him for leading an undemocratic government.

On 2nd March 1955 the young prince, Mahendra Bir Bikram, whose father on his deathbed had conferred full powers on him, reintroduced direct rule. His first act was to take over the actual sovreignty from his dead father after a regency lasting eleven days. Not until 27th January 1956 did Tanka Prasad Acharya form a coalition government at the wish of the king, and he led it until his resignation on 9th July 1957. Then the government was entrusted to K. I. Singh, but as popular protest against the Left Wing United Democratic Party of the latter was too strong, the Cabinet was dismissed on 14th November 1957, and once more the king resorted to direct rule. A Royal Proclamation issued from the Hanuman Dhoka Palace on 12th February was meant to put an end to the ups and downs on the way to a certain kind of democracy. The king proclaimed a Constitution of seventy-seven Articles which promised a bicameral system consisting of a Lower House (Pratinidhi Sabha) and an Upper House (Maha Sabha); also there was to be a Privy Council (Rashtriya Sabha) and a Supreme Court. It seemed that the last lap towards a more or less functional and constitutionally guaranteed administration was assured. Country-wide elections began on 18th February and were concluded in the most outlying corners of the mountain kingdom by 3rd April. The majority of votes were won by the Moderate Socialist Congress Party, whose president was B. P. Koirala. The king entrusted him with the office of Prime Minister on 27th May 1959. For the first time in the history of Nepal the voters had spoken. In his capacity as Prime Minister, Koirala visited India and China, the two great powers who control Nepalese destiny. But the king travelled to the United States and Great Britain (and also incognito to West Germany and other places). In Washington King Mahendra called the prime aim of his foreign policy 'non-alignment and non-entanglement'. But the same year 1960 which had seen in these state visits a hitherto unknown burst of diplomatic activity on the part of Nepal was also to see the end of the Koirala Government. Nepal was in for another spell of royal direct rule. On 15th December the king dismissed the first parliamentary government of the country under B. P. Koirala and had all the ministers arrested. He declared by proclamation that the members of the government had let themselves be influenced by personal interests and had not prepared the economic reconstruction of the country by scientific analysis. This action on the part of the king aroused strong criticism in India. Partisans based on India later tried to overthrow the royal government, which caused severe tension between Katmandu and New Delhi. Furthermore, the rapid construction of a motor road from the capital of Nepal to the capital of Tibet aroused the strongest misgivings in India.

On the other hand, mercenaries in the pay of Great Britain and India provide what is almost the only source of foreign currency for Nepal. After all, there are still twelve Gurkha battalions in the Indian Army and eight Gurkha battalions in the British Army, where they are highly valued as mountain troops. Indeed, their place in British military history can never be usurped, for the Gurkha infantryman with his *kukri* is something for which there is no substitute. In the eyes of the world they are the most obvious representative of the last Hindu monarchy of our times, reigning in the Himalayas under the patronage of Shiva in his aspect 'Pashupatinath'.

Sikkim and Bhutan are monarchies headed by maharajahs, whose political status is, however, different. Whilst Sikkim is an Indian protectorate, Bhutan has the rights of a semi-sovereign state. India exercises suzerainty here: that is to say, she has no sort of influence on internal policy, but represents Bhutan in foreign affairs. As Tibet was for a long period, so today Bhutan is a closed region of Asia.

Bhutan and Sikkim, being two countries in which lamaistic

Buddhism is the state religion, and being neighbours of the Dalai Lama's country, naturally had very close relations with it. Thus even in Sikkim the ruling family, which has reigned there since 1641 and is still reigning today, is descended from the Gyalpos or chiefs of eastern Tibet. For a long time Bhutan was subjected to a double rule, that of a spiritual sovereign, the Shab-tung Rim-po-che or Dharma Rajah, and a temporal lord, the Deb-Rajah. This double rule came to an end after the death in 1904 of the last Dharma Rajah Nga-Wang-Yigmat-Koegyal. The Tongsa Penlop—that was the name for the prime minister—Sir Ugjen Wangchuk, was installed in 1907 as hereditary Maharajah.

Relations between Sikkim and Great Britain were regulated by treaties which brought about the gradual transition of the small maharajah state into a British protectorate. The first treaty with the Rajah of Sikkim was concluded on 10th February 1817. In this agreement the British gave a region which they had taken from the Nepalese, a strip of country between the rivers Mechi and Tista, to the ruler of Sikkim, whom they had just selected to be their protégé in this area. In a decree, called *Sanad*, of 7th April 1817, addressed to the rajah, the new acquisitions finally became the possession of Sikkim. Later the Rajah of Sikkim showed gratitude for these territorial gifts by a return gift: at the request of the British, in a decree published on 1st February 1835, he gave the territory of Darjeeling to the East India Company. The British had selected this lovely spot of God's earth in the midst of the Himalayas as a future 'hill station' for themselves, and it was a foregone conclusion that the rajah should give them the territory. It is true that these gifts of friendship were not always given with a very glad heart, as is shown by the inconsistencies which soon arose. In a treaty dated 28th March 1861, it was therefore laid down how good relations between Gantok, the capital of Sikkim, and Calcutta, the seat of the Governor-General of the East India Company, were to be developed.

On 17th March 1890 Great Britain and China defined in a convention their relationship to Sikkim. In Article 2 of this convention the terms of the British protectorate were clearly laid down:

It is recognized that the British Government, whose protectorate over the state of Sikkim is hereby accepted, possesses direct and exclusive control over the internal administration and the external relations of this state, and that except through and with the consent of the British Government, neither the ruler of the state nor any of its officials may maintain official relations of any kind whatsoever, formal or informal, with any other country.

On 5th December 1950 free India made a treaty with Sikkim by which the relationship of the protectorate to New Delhi was allowed to continue exactly as in the era of the British.

On 11th November 1865, at Sinchula, a treaty had been made with the government of Punakha, the capital of Bhutan. The inhabitants of Bhutan call the document of Sinchula the ten-article treaty of Rawa Pani. According to its conditions Bhutan had to hand over Athara Duras in the foothills of the Himalayas, to the British, who also retain the territories of Assam and Bengali Duras. At the same time Bhutan had to recognize the British as arbitrators if it should have a dispute with the princes of Cooch Behar or Sikkim. For as long as Bhutan kept the treaty, it should receive an annual sum of twenty-five thousand rupees as compensation for the loss of income from the Duras territories. This sum was later to be increased to fifty thousand rupees. At the beginning of this century the relations between Great Britain and Bhutan were once again redefined. On 8th January 1910 the Government of King Edward VII concluded with the *Druk Gyalpo* (the 'King of Thunder') the treaty in which Great Britain undertook not to interfere in the internal administration of Bhutan. In return the foreign policy of Punakha was left entirely to the British. From the British point of view this treaty has been considered rather as an agreement supplementing the arrangements of the Sinchula treaty. On 8th August 1949 the Indian Union concluded the Treaty of Darjeeling with Bhutan, which determined the retention of the old relationship between Punakha and New Delhi which had meanwhile become completely independent.

The Himalayan principalities survive into our own times as a piece of the Asian Middle Ages. Whilst it is very simple to meet these Middle Ages in Nepal, because the Government in Katmandu is friendly to tourists, one cannot unreservedly say the same of the other two countries. It is particularly difficult to reach Bhutan. This is the case not only for Western visitors but also for Indians, whose country has nevertheless the closest relationship with the Himalayan kingdoms. Perhaps the attitude of an Indian journalist, Harish Chandola, may be mentioned here. The statements were made (on 9th February 1958) in an article in the *Times of India* headed (something of a shock to Indian readers): 'Sikkim and Bhutan drift away from India'. Chandola wrote, amongst other things:

My last journey to this state [Sikkim] made me realize what a great influence the changes in Tibet had upon the people of Sikkim. Everywhere along the Indian state road, which runs through Sikkim, everybody was smoking Chinese cigarettes, which were either sold or given to the donkey drivers in Tibet. They showed excitement and curiosity over the changes in Tibet and were full of stories about the results of these changes. In short, their gaze was fixed on Tibet.

Nobody knows what is going on in Bhutan. For India it is a closed country. In spite of our treaty there is no Indian representative in Bhutan. As things are, I do not know whether we can send anybody there at all. No Indian can enter Bhutan without previous written permission from the Bhutanese Government. And nobody receives written permission. In fact, no Indian can ever enter Bhutan.

On the frontiers of this state guards have been posted, who are to seize those who want to force an entry, and throw them out. No Indian representative, even during his official visit, has reached Punakha, the capital of Bhutan. They always met the Maharajah and others in Pharo, half way to Punakha, and then came back. Bhutan's frontiers are its own. We do not know them.

From certain signs outside this state it is clear that we can never really make friends with it. We are as effectively cut off from its people as this mountain race is from us. Officials of Bhutan whom I have met say that the fate of Nepal has taught them a lesson. The attempt to introduce democracy in feudal Nepal has led, according to these Bhutanese officials, to a collapse of its ancient tried and tested form of government.

The old administration has broken down. A new one cannot really take over the task yet, because conditions are not yet ripe for it. The Bhutanese say that they do not wish to repeat this tragedy in their own country. They say they would soon notice it, if one day their people should show themselves open to the revolutionary ideas of democracy.

In Bhutan, too, the Nepalese predominate. There too they form the backbone of the peasant economy of the country. There too discontent is noticeable amongst them. There too we are helpless and must watch whilst our good friends turn to our enemies.

Such articles caused alarm in India. In the course of 1958, Prime Minister Nehru visited Bhutan from 21st to 27th September. But in order to reach this Himalayan country, with its close ties with India, the head of the Indian Government had to take a route over Tibetan territory. After his return there was strong pressure for the construction of a direct motor road from India to Bhutan, which in fact has been built since then. Further ones are planned. In the Himalayas roads are a matter of politics! But politics are not merely a matter of introducing civil engineers to these remote lamaistic kingdoms; all sorts of economic means must contribute to wrench these countries from their seclusion, whether or not there is antagonism between the parties concerned.

In the Himalayas hundreds of races and small nations meet. In them have survived remnants of all the many Tibetan and Mongolian peoples who ever passed through the Himalayan region. To them are added the Indo-Aryan races, who like the Gurkhas later formed the ruling caste. The old races, mostly of Mongolian descent, consist of small communities which are again divided into an endless number of minor races.

But in Nepal there are, of the larger tribes, the Kirat-Rai, Limbu, Magar, Gurung, Tharu, Newar, Sunwar, Dhamang, and finally the 'Eastern people', the Sherpas. In Sikkim one finds the Lepchas, the Mun, Bong-Thing, Rong, Yak-tamba (Limbu), and the Bhodja. Bhutan's tribes include the following: aBrug-pa-Bhodja, Meche, Kachari, Moran and Chutiya.

All these inhabitants of the Himalayas, of whom only a small number in one part of the gigantic range of the Himalayas and their approaches have been mentioned, are people with a view of the world and religious and intellectual ideas which often reach back into the primitive way of thinking of the most distant past. These people live on frontiers which are amongst the most 'sensitive' on earth. It must not be forgotten that the splinter populations inhabiting Soviet Asia, which often spring from the same racial group, were torn out of the past and introduced to the modern age.

Therefore it is worth giving one's whole attention to the problem of the primitive Himalayan peoples and tribes. That can be done only by means of good anthropological groundwork. From this point one can then advance into all the other historical, ethnographical and philosophical fields, as well as those concerning the history of religion and the psychology of race, so as to work out the future treatment of these races. Here I can draw attention to the activity of a new kind of institute, the results of whose labours cannot be overlooked by Himalayan research workers. It is the Anthropos Institute in Bandra, near Bombay, a foundation of the Salesian fathers of the Society of the Divine Word. One of the leading scholars of this project is P. Professor Hermanns, who has written on Chinese and Tibetan subjects in German, Chinese and English, and in 1954 produced a book upon the Indo-Tibetans on the occasion of the one hundred and fifteenth anniversary of the foundation of the Bombay Branch of the Royal Asiatic Society. This unique Anthropos Institute has the following objects: To foster the ethnological and theological investigation of the primitive cultures of India and further the investigation of Indian civilization, with particular reference to its anthropological, ethnological and prehistoric aspects. Previous fields of research have been the racial areas of Nepal, Bhutan, Sikkim, Tibet and Assam. In St Xavier's College instruction in anthropology and ethnology is given by the fathers of the Anthropos Institute. The fact that in addition numerous publications appear, and that suitable Indian collaborators are drawn in, proves how widely felt is the influence of the institute, which is attached to the German religious order.

The three Himalayan principalities are at three different political stages and thus have three different kinds of relationships with their neighbours. Somehow they form vacuums, they are borderlands in their many different levels of associations to the north and to the south. Borderlands can unite, separate or ward off. Nepal's gaze turns towards India and the south, the two other principalities look south in politics and north in their religious concerns. Out of the knowledge of such tensions arises the interest which is bestowed on the last Hindu and lamaistic monarchies.

Mr Nehru, Prime Minister of India, with U Nu, then Prime Minister of Burma, at a reception of Buddhists from all over south-east Asia at Sanchi in Central India, 1952.

The Dalai Lama, right, garlanded, and the High Lama of Ladakh, centre, behind plant at a Tree Planting Ceremony. Left, the author

5

Disharmony in Assam

MOUNTAIN TRIBES IN THE OIL COUNTRY DISCOVER THEMSELVES

THE most eastern member state of the Indian Union lies hemmed in between Burma, East Pakistan, China, Tibet and Bhutan. Only a narrow corridor forms its link with the rest of India, with the neighbouring state of West Bengal. Even this brief geographical indication of Assam's position shows how exceptional its situation is. There is something else exceptional about the region of Assam as compared with other Indian lands—if I may be allowed, for the sake of simplicity, to apply this idea geographically and not politically, and extend it to include the states of Manipur and Tripura and also the border territories of the race not subject to the government of Assam: Assam was directly acquainted with the events of the Second World War.

When the Japanese proclaimed their gospel of *Dai To-a Kyoeiken* ('Greater East Asian Sphere of Prosperity'), and, in the course of the hostilities, the 'provisional government of Free India', formed in Singapore by supporters of the circle around Subhas Chandra Bose on 21st October 1943, addressed itself to the Indian provinces and states, India had become one of the great prizes of the war in Asia. The Indian National Army—*Azad Hind Fauj*—formed in Malaya and Burma followed in the wake of the Japanese attack as far as Imphal in the state of Manipur. Assam had already been abandoned and the British headquarters, which were in

Ranchi, were already expecting an attack on Bengal, the home of Bose.

In the end matters did not get so far, but the fact that the Japanese occupied Burma and the adjoining Indian zone was for long enough to be quoted as the reason for the unrest which seized individual tribes in India and Burma just at the time when both these states had become masters of their own destiny.

The Indians were accustomed to look again and again to the north-west of their country, where conquerors could make a way into the plain of the Ganges. But the Second World War pointed out the other gateway to India in the north-eastern corner. Today the keys of the north-west lie in the hand of Pakistan, but security of the north-east is an Indian task.

Assam, the country on the Brahmaputra, or upper Assam, and on the River Surma (lower Assam), is India in miniature. In upper Assam live the Assamiya-speaking inhabitants of the country, from whom it takes its name. Lower Assam is like a second Bengal. In the past there were many frictions between the Assamiya- and Bengali-speaking inhabitants. Amongst the former the fear prevailed that the cultural predominance of the language of Tagore might be too strong. On the other hand they pleaded strongly for their own province, Purvachal. Today these aims have by no means been abandoned.

The geographical area 'Assam' is the home of many tribes. The very history of this country is the chronicle of tribal rule, the most famous of which was Pragjyotisa, with its capital Pragjyotisapura near Gauhati. Somewhere in the seventh century there flourished the kingdom of Kamarupa, which was known even in China as Kamolupo, and amongst Iranian and Arab writers as Kamru or Kamrat. When the Shans had set out in the thirteenth century from the central areas of lower India to conquer what was later to become Assam, they perhaps gave the country its present name at the same time. In the Thai language *cham* means 'conquered' and, in conjunction with the Aryan prefix *a-*, *acham* would mean the 'unconquered'. Now whether the Shans brought a Thai name with them, or whether the Boro name for 'low country', *hacom*, is the root of the word Assam, may be of no consequence. However, the philological explanation can often throw light on psychological connections between the former conquerors and the conquered. The kingdom of the Shans, then known as Ahom, which had defended itself so successfully against the Moghuls, had to yield to the British in 1826. By the Peace of Jandabu, which opened the road to Burma to the British, Assam was added to the mighty realm of the East India Company.

Here in the valleys Aryan civilization once clashed with more Eastern non-Aryan cultures. This can be traced not only in many Tantrian rites and in the belief in magic, but also even in the vocabulary.

To mention only one example: there are almost always in the Assamese language two words for groups of people, according to whether younger or older ones are meant. Thus the elder brother is called *Kakai* and the younger *Bhai*. The former word is not Indoeuropean, but the latter is. This kind of double designation, typical of a region of cultural synthesis, runs through the whole language.

In Assam, where the Indoeuropean, Austrish and Tibetan-Burmese worlds touch, there was also a meeting of religious movements. There is scarcely one religious sentiment, ranging from the animistic, the cult of fertility or the Hindu longing for God, to that of an Islamic or Christian faith, which could not be traced in Assam, the Land of Transit and at the same time the place of assembly.

Assam is the centre of a silk industry which has been worked for centuries and which has brought much money into the country. In the last century it was developed into the tea garden of India. And finally it is today the oil country of the Indian subcontinent. About four hundred and fifty thousand barrels of crude oil are obtained every year near Digboi and Nahorkatiya. However, the whole of India needs more than five million barrels annually. The great oil centres of the Near East and Caucasia, Rumania, Venezuela and the United States can naturally supply many times this amount, which in India is still a dream of the economists. But the stimulus has been supplied to carry out further research in different parts of the country, in order to discover new sources. The eastern state of the republic is an important factor in the plan for Indian industrialization.

All these plans are made for the river valleys. In the hill country, where the tribes live, the preoccupation is not with the industrial future but with political problems.

Tribal cultures always take precedence over other questions, as the regions of civilization which find their expression in cities. In the case of the former everything is embedded in a traditional order, whilst in the cities people attain intellectual and political individuality, different points of view and attitudes. Thus there arose a clash between the tribal village in the hills and the seats of government on the rivers which linked the towns. The Nagas were the first of the tribes to discover themselves and to be seized by unrest.

This unrest of the Nagas, which ended in a bitter and bloody battle, was concerned with the preservation of their ancient tribal culture, including language, customs and traditions and religious practices. The Nagas regard the institution of the *Morung* as the greatest achievement of their social order. This is the bachelors' hall, where the unmarried male Nagas have their living and sleeping quarters. Amongst a section of the Nagas, the Ao and the Lotha, this institution is tending to disappear. On the other hand it can be observed amongst the other sections that the Morung is exercising an increased attraction, and that a great deal is done in it for the education of the Nagas in their old tribal customs. Just because the Morung are of the greatest significance in the life of the Nagas, it might be permissible to quote here an authority on the Nagas, S. Wati Aonok. Excerpts from his articles which appeared on 10th June 1956 in the *Hindustan Standard* give an idea of the significance of the Morung as one of the pillars of the Naga culture and its organization built upon the tradition of communal work.

The word 'Morung' is not a Naga name. The Ao-Nagas call it *Arejo*, the Lotha-Nagas *Champo*, the Rengma-Nagas *Rensi*, the Angami-Nagas *Kitchuki*, the Chang-Nagas *Haghe* and the Nokte-Nagas *Poh*. The Morung has no meaning at all in the village of the Angami, and it is practically unknown amongst the Sema-Nagas. In the first case some private house or other, and in the second the chief's house, fulfil the purpose of a Morung. A close investigation reveals the striking similarity between the Morung organizations amongst the Konyak-Nagas, the Chang-Nagas and the Nokte-Nagas. Amongst the Ao-Nagas the Morung was once the most remarkable institution and played the most important part in the social life of the village. I should also like to point out that amongst the Ao-Nagas the Morung surpassed all others in its structure, organization and in its strict laws.

The Morung is the most remarkable part of the life of the Nokte-Nagas. It is in the Morung that the old men tell of the great deeds of the past, and that the coming generation is taught to live in the future in the way of the old tradition. It is a place of instruction for youth. Leadership is in the hands of two or three of the young men, who are exempt from fetching water and fuel. Here a boy learns to grow up healthy in body and mind, he learns to become a member of his tribe, and here he is best accustomed to discipline. His judgment is sharpened and his abilities reach their height. He is no longer a child who must be supervised by his parents—he assumes the obligations and the virtues of a hunter. If it is not so there is no place for him in the Morung.

The Morung is a guard-house. In the good old days when head-hunting was still the custom, the Morung served as the village guard-house. . . . It is at the same time the place where the skulls are kept. Attacks were planned and discussed here and all skulls won were brought here. . . . A Morung is at the same time a sanctuary. Even a criminal, whether he belongs to the village or is a fugitive from another one, cannot be seized while he is seeking refuge in the Morung. . . . It is a club for men, which no woman may enter. . . . Moreover the Morung is a place where working songs, love, dance, ritual, hunting and war songs are taught and learnt. In this way the tradition in the songs is preserved. . . .

Nagaland was divided into three administrative districts: the Naga mountain district, as a part of Assam, the Tuensang-Tirap region and a small strip in the state of Manipur. In addition there are also numerous Nagas living across the Burmese frontier.

The territory of the Nagas and of many other tribes had formerly been closed to the British in comparison with the rest of India. It was impossible to enter the territory without special permission. It was the home of an ancient tribal culture, whose fortified settlements reflected the warlike character of the inhabitants. In the middle of the last century many regions of Nagaland were considered very dangerous because the dreaded head-hunters lived there.

There was constant unrest here. In 1839 the British sent out the first punitive expedition to bring the Nagas under control. In the mid sixties the dissatisfaction of the Nagas reached its peak. Conditions were chaotic and the British decided to take a step which was to give the Nagas the feeling that they could manage their own tribal affairs, and at the same time make it possible to control them. In 1866 they created a district of the 'Naga Hills'. The seat of this administrative region of the Naga mountain territory was in Samaguting, and in 1874, after Assam had become a Chief Commissioner's Province, it was moved to Kohima, the centre of the Angami-Nagas. Nevertheless peace and order did not come even after the establishment of administrative unity for Nagaland. Rather there were violent risings against the British, and in 1879 and 1880 the rebellion started with one of the Naga tribes, the Angami. The village of Khonoma was the centre of the movement against the British. After these disturbances the territory of the Nagas was increased still more by the addition of strips of land inhabited by Nagas but so far not subject to control—as, for example, the area of the Ao-Nagas, who in 1890 were able to enjoy the blessings of modern administration. Finally, after 1947, there was created the so-called Tuensang Frontier Division in the North-East Frontier Agency, the frontier territory under the direct control of Delhi.

The disruption of Nagaland has been partly responsible for the present unrest. But of course there was something else. After the departure of the British, some of the Naga leaders felt a vacuum. They had been treated by the British just like tribes who are condemned as savages.

However, there had also been many changes in Nagaland. Christian missionaries had not only brought their faith to the members of the Naga and other mountain and frontier tribes of Assam, but had also taught them to write their own language in Roman letters. In addition, it happened that because of the collapse of the Japanese Great East Asian Empire, many weapons from the remnants of the Japanese forces fell suddenly into the hands of the border tribes.

Khonoma had already once played a part in the history of the Naga people, and it regained its importance in the first decade of India's freedom. From this village comes Zapu Phizo, who made himself spokesman for the discontented amongst the Nagas. The claims of these extremists went so far that they demanded an independent and sovereign Nagaland. For years battles flared up and died down again. Finally, in the summer of 1957, there came the famous Kohima Convention, which was attended by 1,735 delegates from the different tribes of the Konyak, Chang, Phom, Sangtam, Yimchungurr, Sema and Khiemyungam, the Angami, Chakasang, Lotha, Ao, Zeliang, Rengma, Kuki, Kachari and Mikir. At this conference, which was attended especially by the supporters of the moderate line, the desire of the Nagas to live in a Naga district of their own was expressed. In the Indian Parliament, Lok Sabha, the law uniting the Nagas hills district and the Naga territory of Tuensang was quickly passed and the new Naga Region came into existence on 1st December 1957.

This measure, which to be sure did not immediately make moderate Nagas out of extremists, had shown what great importance was attached to Assam. When the sixty-third annual assembly of the Indian National Congress (the movement which had led the struggle for Indian freedom) took place at the beginning of 1958 near Gauhati—the meeting-place was given the name of Pragjyotishpur in memory of the old capital—the main subject for discussion was suddenly the question of the national language. This subject depends upon the structure of the state just as does every tendency towards greater political self-sufficiency.

The events in the region of Kohima-Mokokchung, which in August 1957 led to the formation of the Naga People's Convention, were due to the initiative of a Dr Inkongliba Ao, an opponent of A. Z. Phizo, the later president of the Naga 'Interim' Council. His efforts were crowned with success when on 1st August 1960 Prime Minister Nehru announced the formation of a new administrative unit, the State of Nagaland, in the Indian House of Commons. But Dr Inkongliba Ao himself was to suffer for the insecurity of his fellow-tribesmen and their shuttlecock attitude, alternating between radicalism and conservatism. He fell victim to an assassin. He was attacked on 22nd August 1961 and died two days later, a great loss to the Moderate Party among Nagas, as well as to New Delhi, which has not devoted sufficient care to the problem of the North-East Frontier region.

The problem, which also made the solution of the Naga question more difficult, is the possible effect on the other tribes. There are so many of them. They are settled in strategically important parts of the country, where the Japanese attacks during the Second World War robbed the Assamese jungle of its reputation for impenetrability.

But on the other hand the Russians and the government of the Chinese People's Republic carry on skilful propaganda. They spread the view that they have solved the problem of introducing tribes to a modern civilization in such a way that tribal culture, tradition and language are preserved. This was the second reason which gave the disturbances amongst a small people numbering scarcely four hundred thousand a world-wide political significance. And when one reads the commentaries in the publications of the Indian Communists, every politically interested person in the West can only hope that India will soon overcome the difficulties in her problem state of Assam.

6

Burmese Elegy

A LAND DREAMS AWAY ITS BUDDHIST KINGDOM OF PEACE

THE ideal of the state of the ancient kingdom of Burma sprang from India's spiritual ground. It made the ruler the instrument for fulfilment of the divine will. But the king himself spoke for the god Indra—called *Shakra* in Burma. For the inhabitants of Burma, Indra was the lord of the mythical mountain Meru, and it is curious that in Buddhism, which originally arose as a reaction against the belief in the gods, this home of the heavenly ones became the model for the Burmese royal palace. The royal residence in Mandalay was held to be the earthly embodiment of the sacred mountain. The king was the representative upon earth of the god Indra and bore the title Chakravartin, which lives in the Buddhist philosophy of the state. Buddha's teaching and faith in God combined in the longing for a Buddhist world empire.

For that reason one of the formal titles of the ruler of Mandalay was 'Centre of the Cosmos'. Another form of ceremonial address was 'King, leader of men and gods across the rushing stream of suffering to the silent island of peace'. This Hindu-Buddhist conception of the king is spread through the whole of the Indian interior. In the kingdom of Fu-nan, which lasted in Cochin China from the first to the sixth century, there were rulers with the title *Sailendra*, which means 'mountain king' and indicates Mount Meru. The word 'Fu-nan' itself might be the translation of the king's title, which came from India, but *bnan* means 'mountain'

63

in the Khmer language. In the reign of Jayavarman II in the ninth century, Cambodia accepted the idea of world empire and divine kingship. In the eighth century Javanese kings assumed the Sailendra title of the Fu-nan rulers, in order to announce their claim to world rule. Thus the spiritual influence of the Himalayas was long felt in the whole sphere of syncretist Hindu-Buddhist culture. In the Western world there was at one time a separation between the imperial temporal power and the spiritual papal power. In the interior of India, on the contrary, spiritual and temporal rule were combined in the king. In order to give priestly consecration to the divine kingship, which was unlike Buddhism in its appeal to gods, the god-king rulers of Central India made sure of the help of Brahmins in their royal ritual.

The justification of the ideal of Chakravartin was the rulers' duty to preserve peace for all men. It arose from the conception of the duty of the head of state.

When the new republic of Burma had established itself a little, its statesmen announced the construction of the Kaba-E pagoda, the Buddhist pagoda of world peace. At the same time the Sixth Great Buddhist Council, Chattha Sangayana, was summoned to Rangoon.

It is possible to trace the main thread of a political and spiritual aim of Chakravartin, both in the goal of the kings, and in the republican programme of Burma's former and present rulers. They are the expression of a longing for peace, which is no Utopian ideal of the state, proclaiming the unattainable in sparkling words. It is a sign of the attitude of the Burmese people. Above all, it is dictated by necessity arising from the situation of the country and then drawing the political moral.

Burma is a country with a definite agricultural pattern. The industry of its rural population once made it the rice bowl of southeast Asia, and rice is still today amongst the chief exports of the country. Its rulers chose the road of Socialism to lead the land from the era of peasant culture into the age of modern technology. But one cannot compare the Burmese Socialists with those of Europe without some qualification. The inherited tradition of Buddhism is much too strong for that. The Prime Minister, U Nu, once coined the phrase that the dust under Buddha's feet was worth more than all the knowledge of Karl Marx. That shows how Buddhism and Socialism are to be ranged in the Burman's scale of values. One cannot without further consideration choose the simplified formula, 'Buddha plus Marx equals the new Burma'.

Burma lies on the frontier between two spheres of influence and in addition between two great states. It is on the borders of Pakistan, which is linked by military alliance with Turkey and Iran to the Near Eastern security system, the Bagdad Pact countries which were deprived of their Arabian partner by the Iraki revolution of 14th July 1958; Burma also has a common frontier with Siam, which belongs to the Far Eastern Manila defence area of the West. Pakistan likewise belongs to the latter. But to the north lies Communist China, and the other frontier neighbour is India. These two are as regards population the biggest countries on earth, in comparison with which Burma, with scarcely twenty million inhabitants, is only a small state. In the east the state of Laos, which the present world situation has long kept divided, has dedicated itself to a neutrality again completely different from that of other states in the Indian and south-east Asian sphere.

In Burma the much-emphasized friendship with her over-populated neighbours cannot dispel a certain amount of mistrust. The large Indian and Chinese minorities in the towns create plenty of political problems. The greatest wealth of the country is in the hands of the Burman Chinese. Some of the most prosperous newspapers have Chinese backing. In addition the present governing class in Burma knows that Communism is the greatest enemy of their country, which since 1948 has been free of all commitments. The rebellion of the Communists, who understood how to combine their goal of world revolution with the national aims of the Karen tribe, showed that very clearly. A definite policy of neutrality is intended to deter the Communists from their seditious work. Burma has no need of two things: the all-too-powerful wooing of over-populated countries who could direct their surplus populations still more into the fertile rice-growing plains: nor does she need their enmity. Nevertheless the nature of her relations with her neighbours is quite different. In the Burmese language the Chinese are called *pauk-hpaw*. This word has a second meaning: 'the friend'. It is the same with the word for 'Indian' (*Kala*), but the second meaning here is 'stranger'. This clearly reveals the influence and predominance of the East Asian world of ideas in Burma. It should not be forgotten that although the state of Burma belongs geographically entirely to the Indian and south-east Asian sphere, and is part of the monsoon area affected by the Indian Ocean, it was, until the beginning of the British era, under the control of the Middle Kingdom, even if this control was in part only nominal. In the different provinces of daily life one can trace the preponderance of the Sino-Asiatic culture. It begins with certain foods, then passes by way of the regard for silk clothing to the importance which is attached to jade, for example, that typical Chinese precious stone. In addition there are the relations with Buddhism, in which the great dividing lines between Hinayana and Mahayana are willingly overlooked.

Buddhism is still the motive force in Burma. The identification between Buddhism and government is far-reaching.[1] It is like the situation in Europe in the Middle Ages. For example, today if a Burmese *Thera*, that is a Buddhist abbot, can prove that he knows the Buddha canon, the *Tiptikas*, by heart, he is entitled to the free use of all means of transport, including aeroplanes. All means of land transport are likewise made freely available to other Buddhist *Sayadaws* (monks with the titles Abhi Dhaja Maha Guru and Agga Maha Pandita).

It was the simple, uncomplicated attitude to daily problems which inspired Article 211 of the Burmese Constitution, without doubt dictated out of genuine love of peace: 'The union of the states of Burma rejects war as an instrument of national policy and accepts the universally acknowledged principles of international law as the basis of negotiations with foreign countries.' However, Article 212 of the Burmese Constitution reads: 'The union of the states of Burma affirms its devotion to the ideal of friendly co-operation between the nations, based upon international justice and morality.' The creators of these principles, who were inspired by high morality, will doubtless be asked what 'international justice' or 'international morality' is. Our world is the battleground for intrigues and struggles for power. Burma came to feel this in her internal affairs when the (largely Christian) Karens began the revolt which is still kept going by the Communists; she also felt it in external relations. In the north the problem was for a long time an area occupied by the Red Chinese. After long pressure here Burma was obliged to yield some regions

[1] In 1961 Buddhist monks demonstrated violently when the Government passed the Act of Toleration for other sects.

to the Chinese. That such events are noted even in Asia is shown by the document *Chinese 'Panch-Shila' in Burma,* by Girilal Jain, in which Peking's attitude is sharply criticized. Another matter, this time affecting the Russians, annoyed the Burmans greatly. When the Soviet leaders Khrushchev and Bulganin visited India, Burma and Afghanistan in 1955, there began for the Government in Rangoon the tragic chapter of diplomacy concerned with rice and roubles which disillusioned them more and more.

On their return from Asia Khrushchev and Bulganin had reported success before the Supreme Soviet. In Bulganin's speech, published in *Pravda* on 30th December 1955, he said:

We have reached an agreement that the Soviet Union will co-operate in the establishment of the programme for agricultural development, in the most important works of irrigation and in the building and construction of some industrial enterprises. Burma for her part will sell rice to the Russians, and in case the quantity of rice for sale does not cover the value of our deliveries, Burma will claim the right of credit, that is to say, will openly arrange to make payments in kind over a period of years.

As a sign of goodwill and respect for the people of the Union of Burma we have, in the name of and commissioned by the Government of the Soviet Union, offered the Burmese Union, as a gift, to build and establish, out of the strength and resources of the Union of Socialist Soviet Republics, a technological institute in Rangoon. The Government of the Union of Burma fully appreciates the motives of the Soviet Government in making this offer, and has accepted the gift with deep gratitude to the Soviet Government and people. In the name of the people of the Union of Burma, the Prime Minister, U Nu, has for his part offered as a gift to the Soviet Union a corresponding quantity of rice and certain other goods of Burmese origin. In the name of the people of the Soviet Union we have accepted this gift with gratitude.

Bulganin, who was at that time still basking in the glory of the office of Soviet Prime Minister, here began a chapter which was to cause much bad blood in Burma. The Russians had taken from the Government in Rangoon a large quantity of rice, and in Burma people had rejoiced at the prospect of having obtained a new and well-paying purchaser for the coming years. When the Burmese made the trade agreement with the Russians, the price of rice stood at 495 Kyat a ton. But it soon rose to 1,000 Kyat. The Burmese were obliged to deliver at the lower price. However, they hoped for foreign currency from the other rice-importing countries, amongst them Ceylon. But one could picture the amazement in Rangoon when it was announced in Colombo that the Russians were delivering rice to them in the near future. The rice handed over to the Russians by the Burmese, which was intended to enrich the Soviet menu, was delivered to Ceylon: of course this was delivered at the higher price! At the same time the Russians had promised the Burmese a technical college. 'For nothing! We do this for our friends. The Burmese must allow us one thing only: to put up a tablet stating that this college is a gift from the people of the Soviet Union to the people of Burma,' Khrushchev had said.

Nevertheless the Prime Minister, U Nu, had declared that the Burmese did not want gifts, and therefore the Russians were to accept the rice as a return gift. And so the Russians delivered the gifts as a 'rescue operation' from which they obtained full propaganda value in every way and moreover accepted payment for them. These deliveries to Burma were part of the Soviet economic global offensive which was intended to demonstrate to the technically underdeveloped countries the usefulness of friendship with the Soviet Union. Thus the Russians sought by every means to increase the volume of trade of these countries with the states of the Soviet bloc. It was all the easier to exert a certain political pressure. The Burmese soon came to realize that the possibilities of this economic help are of course limited for the time being by the capacity of the Russians.

In the Burmese schools and technical colleges of the Union of Burma (the latter bear significantly the name of *Tekkatho* and recall the Buddhist Graeco-Bactrian Indian *Taxila*, thus forming an intellectual bridge between the western and eastern foothills of the Himalayas) young people are growing up educated completely in the spirit of Buddhism, but in addition coming to terms with Marxism also. In the country itself, over-rapid socialization has brought many tensions in the economic sphere, which could lead to internal danger. It is self-evident that in an unindustrialized Asiatic country, industrialization must be handled carefully and not according to the economic pattern of any Western state, where such measures are set in motion in accordance with the laws of free competition and private enterprise. Nevertheless, in the opinion of a number of experts, socialization in Burma was too severe. And so new laws are to encourage new investment of private capital.

Burma has found it easier than India has to solve one of its major problems, that of the frontier with China. On 28th January 1960 a treaty of friendship was drawn up between China and India based on the five principles for friendly co-existence (*Panch-Shila*) and appealing to the ten principles of the Bandung Conference. In India mention of the five principles in this connection was looked on as provocation. Of late years there has been a noticeable increase in the sphere of religious activity on the part of the Burmese Government. There was a desire to stabilize the situation by means of a law making Buddhism the established religion. In fact such a law came into force on 26th August 1961, but official pronouncements denied that any other doctrine was thereby discredited or intended to be placed at any disadvantage. On the other hand, the state had the duty of constituting the pillar of Buddhist doctrine, as it had already been in the days of the Burmese monarchy. The rights of religious minorities were defined in a law of 25th September in the same year.

In the administrative field, however, greater uncertainty prevailed, showing itself in the still unresolved struggle between military and political leaders. On 28th October 1958, three weeks after the military coup at Karachi and the day before the take-over of power by General Ayub Khan in the dual state of Pakistan, General Ne Win took over the powers of government in Rangoon and still retains them, despite a few political intermezzos.

The Burmese are proud of the fact that U Thant was elected secretary-general of the United Nations, and hastened to confer on him the resounding and fascinating title of Thado Thiri Thudamma. But at the same time less pleasant tasks had to be performed in Rangoon, such as the stabilizing of finance and economy.

However, Burma has to face her greatest battle not in the economic but in the political field. The tug-of-war between the great powers and their political ideologies has thrown this country, which once dedicated itself so zealously to the Buddhist ideal of peace, into a state of uncertainty which often assumes an ominous note, placed as it is on one of the most 'sensitive' frontiers of our time. The struggle in and for Burma began with the internal political fight when on 19th July 1947, shortly before the recovery of their freedom, a murderous fusillade of sub-machine guns carried off at one blow the whole of the provisional government.

Catastrophe seemed unavoidable. It was a miracle that nevertheless political leaders were found to carry on to the end of the road, to the proclamation of an independent Burma. In external affairs the struggle continues—not surrounded by so much drama and glaring sensationalism, but nevertheless having unique significance for the whole of south-east Asia.

House-boats on
the River Jhelun
in Kashmir

View from Dar-
jeeling towards
Kanchenjunga

7

Pakistan's Vision

THE MYTH OF THE HIMALAYAS
TRANSLATED INTO ISLAMIC TERMS

ON THE frontier of Kashmir, in Sialkot in the Punjab, on 22nd
February 1873, was born Mohammed Iqbal, who was to become
a heaven-sent poet and the prophet of the idea of a state of Islam.
In three languages, Urdu, Persian and English, he wrote and
thought and demonstrated to his fellow countrymen with great
power of conviction the vision of a future state of Pakistan.

The Himalayan glaciers gleamed near Iqbal's home. There,
between the sacred rivers of the Indus and the Ganges, the young
Mohammed felt for the first time the breadth of the Indian cosmos,
with exactly the same ardent feeling as meditating Brahmins,
whom Iqbal was always proud to call his ancestors; but later he
was drawn more and more to the manliness of the Islamic faith
and the struggle of Western philosophy with its devotion to freedom and human dignity. This Indian Westerner, who studied in
India and England, and later at Heidelberg and Munich, where
he wrote his thesis upon *The Development of Metaphysics in Persia*,
was at once a citizen of the world and the child of his native
land. But he was especially a citizen of the future state of Pakistan.

Again and again he looked to the centre of the continent of Asia
—Iqbal belonged to that generation which saw its own state embedded in the larger Asia. At some time in the future the gospel
of freedom was to be proclaimed to the whole earth from the

centre of Asia, from the Himalayas. And he wanted to rise up and help. 'The heart of Asia is enclosed in a hard shell and I want to break it,' he once proclaimed.

Millions and millions of his Hindu fellow countrymen gazed towards the Himalayas. They felt at home there. It was their intellectual and spiritual home.

And the Moslem Iqbal gazed towards the Himalayas also, but not with the enraptured gaze of the pilgrim. As a politician he saw in the Himalayas a great fortress to protect the land of India. The poet in him gladly accepted the idea that heaven had created this castle and rampart for that reason only: 'Ai Himala! Ai Fasil-e-kishware Hindustan Chumta hai teri Peshani ko jhuk kar Asman.' ('O Himalayas! You are the strong rampart of the kingdom of India. Heaven bows down to kiss your brow.')

He wrote these words when, feeling himself completely Indian, he simply could not withdraw from his experience of the Himalayas. And he celebrates the most sacred of all sacred rivers in similar terms. He dedicates these lines to the Ganges, the dearest child of the Himalayas: 'Ay ab-e-rode Ganga wo din hain yad tujh ko, Utra tere kinare jab karavan hamara?' ('Oh you waters of the Ganges, do you remember those days when our caravan reached your shores?')

Iqbal was a true son of the Indian world in its striving after the universe, after the highest, which found its expression in the Himalayas. The poet of Pakistan has translated the myth of the Himalayas into Islamic. In addition to breadth of religious vision he possessed political insight. But the man who was at the same time mystic and politician, who on the one hand shattered Indian unity but on the other spoke of the still greater Asiatic unity, was more than a mere Pakistani politician. He was a universalist. He regarded, as his ultimate goal, the universe in which faith in equality of rights for men and hope for a world filled with deep self-confidence would operate. Thus Iqbal was also convinced that communities should first of all find themselves and then work in larger units. In this belief he was full of confidence that Asia would one day occupy a position of power upon earth which would enable it to utter a decisive—perhaps *the* decisive—word in current events. Iqbal's spiritual and political world was revealed particularly clearly in his *Javid-Nameh*, the translation of which, by Anne-Marie Schimmel, with the title *Buch der Ewigkeit* ('Book of Eternity') was issued in 1957 in the publications of the German Institute for Foreign Relations.

The poet and philosopher, who died on 21st April 1938, and the anniversary of whose death is celebrated every year as 'Iqbal Day' in the whole of Pakistan, declared in 1930 in his opening address as president of the Moslem League:

I should very much like to see Punjab, the North-West Frontier Province, Sind and Baluchistan combined in one single province. Whether there is self-government within the Commonwealth or outside this union of the British family of nations, the creation of a united Moslem state seems to me to be the highest aim of the Moslem in India. This idea need disturb neither the Hindus nor the British. The life of Islam as a cultural force depends largely upon its centralization in one definite region.

Next to Iqbal, the mystic and politician, one must mention Rahmat Ali, and above all Mohammed Ali Jinnah, who wanted to give political form to the idea of Pakistan. The word Pakistan is often interpreted in different ways. The translation is said to be 'Land of the Pure'. On the other hand, it is an acrostic made up from Punjab, Afghan North-West Frontier Province, Kashmir, Sind and Baluchistan. On 23rd March 1940, at an historic meeting of the Moslem League, Pakistan was proclaimed as a political demand. This significant resolution at Lahore ran as follows:

It is the general opinion of this session of the All-Indian Moslem League that no constitutional plan in this country can be workable or acceptable to the Moslems unless it is based upon the following principles, i.e.: Geographically connected units are to be declared regions which shall be so constituted that after the necessary territorial changes, the districts in which Moslems are numerically a majority should be grouped to form independent states, in which the essential units should be autonomous and sovereign.

Appropriate, effective and firmly established protection shall be specially provided in the constitution for the minorities in the individual states and regions, to safeguard their religious, cultural, economic, political, constitutional and other rights and interests, after consultation with them; and in other parts of India where Moslems are in a minority, appropriate, effective and firmly established protection shall be specially provided in the constitution for them and other minorities, to safeguard their religious, cultural, economic, political, constitutional and other rights and interests, after consultation with them. Further, the Congress authorizes the executive committee to formulate the plan for a constitution in harmony with these basic principles. Finally, precautions shall be taken in the regions concerned to take over the arrangements for defence, the foreign service, trade, customs and other ministries considered necessary.

While discussing the historical origin of the name and conception of Pakistan, may I finally draw attention to the book *Inside India*, which appeared in London in 1937. The authoress of this book is a Turkish writer, Halidé Edib, and she gives us the following answer from the mouth of Ali Rahmat to the question 'How did the Pakistan National Movement arise?' The claim which Rahmat makes, to be the creator of the word 'Pakistan', is indeed remarkable:

I should have to go over the history of the past eighty years in order to give a satisfactory answer. The Moslem empire collapsed in 1857. With regard to the Indian Moslems there is one point—a very important point—which is not seen quite clearly abroad. First of all it must be stated that the Moslems had their home in Pakistan, that is to say, the Punjab, in the North-West Frontier Province (also called the Afghan Province) in Kashmir, Sind and Baluchistan—I made up the name Pakistan out of the names of these five provinces. The Moslems lived there for more than two hundred years and had their own history, civilization and culture. The region is separated from India proper—Hindustan—by the River Jumna; and it is not a part of India. Although more than twelve hundred years ago Hindus were there, and a Hindu empire, since 712, that is, for far more than a thousand years, they, the Hindus, have been a minority group.

The total population of Pakistan is forty-two millions, of whom thirty-two millions are Moslems. Their racial origins are to be found in Central Asia, and they are different sociologically and their type of civilization is completely different from that of Hindustan. Islam as a social, moral and political system is the key to the nation of Pakistan, and is the predominant characteristic of this nation. I should like you to recognize this basic fact quite clearly, madam. The Moslems of Hindustan, that is of India proper, came there as conquerors. Therefore Hindustan was the Moslem empire, where they ruled as a native majority for more than nine hundred years. But when they lost this colonial empire, which differs in this way from Pakistan, the Moslems who had settled in these Moslem imperial domains became a minority group in Hindustan. I have nothing to say against it: it is a fact.

It is a surprising fact that in the first discussions about a future state of Pakistan, East Bengal was never mentioned, nor was Mohammedanism in general in eastern India. However, in 1937, Iqbal, a year before his death, and Mohammed Ali Jinnah, who as head of the Moslem League bore the title 'Quaid-i-Azam', that is, 'great leader', put the question: 'Why should not the Moslems of North-West India and Bengal be regarded as nations which have the right of self-determination just like other nations in and outside India?' With that the problem of a double state of Pakistan was raised.

Pakistan as an idea and an actuality was of course violently attacked by the Congress Party. But they would not admit that the Moslems wanted to fight a battle for freedom, in order then to create their own state. Even on 6th April 1940 Gandhi wrote in his journal *Harijan*:

But I do not believe that, if it ever comes to an actual decision, the Moslems will agree to a division into two parts. Their good sense will prevent them. Their self-interest will deter them. Their religion will forbid the obvious suicide which the division means. The 'two nations' theory is an untruth. The great majority of Moslems in India have been converted to Islam or are descendants of converts. They did not become a new nation as soon as they were converted. . . .

Shortly after the end of the Second World War a British Cabinet mission went to India. On 16th May 1946 the political problem of India was dealt with in a joint statement by the mission and by the viceroy. In it great attention was paid to the complex question of Pakistan. This declaration states amongst other things:

If the internal peace of India is to be secured, it must be secured by measures in which Moslems are assured of control in all vital questions of their culture, religion and economy and other interests.

Therefore we have first of all examined the question of a separate and fully independent sovereign state of Pakistan. Such a state of Pakistan would include two regions, one in the north-west, consisting of the provinces of Punjab, Sind, North-West Frontier and British Baluchistan; the other in the north-east consisting of the provinces of Bengal and Assam. The League has declared itself prepared to accept frontier changes at a later date, but insists first of all upon a recognition in principle of the demand for a state of Pakistan.

The argument for a separate state of Pakistan is based in the first place upon the right of the Moslem majority to decide their form of government in accordance with their wishes, and then upon the necessity to incorporate essential regions in which Moslems are in a minority, so as to make Pakistan capable of administration and economically viable. . . .

(The declaration then gave a table of the population, according to the census of 1941, calculating for the north-western provinces 22,653,294 Moslems (62·07 per cent) and 13,840,231 non-Moslems (37·93 per cent), and for the north-eastern provinces 36,447,913 Moslems (51·69 per cent) and 34,064,345 non-Moslems (48·31 per cent). There then remained a minority of about 20 million Moslems in the rest of India!)

These figures show that the creation of a separate sovereign state of Pakistan, as the Moslem League demands, will in no way solve the problem of minorities. We can also find no justification for incorporating in a sovereign Pakistan those districts of Punjab and Bengal and Assam in which the population is preponderantly non-Mohammedan. Every argument which can be used in favour of Pakistan can equally be applied in favour of excluding these districts from Pakistan. In particular this point concerns the position of the Sikhs.

We had therefore considered as a possible compromise a small sovereign state of Pakistan, merely limited to the regions with a majority of Moslems. The setting up of such a state of Pakistan was regarded by the Moslem League as completely unworkable, because it would lead to the exclusion from Pakistan of the following regions: (a) the entire districts of Ambala and Jullundur in the Punjab; (b) the whole of Assam with the exception of the district of Sylhet; (c) a large part of West Bengal, including Calcutta, where Moslems make up 23·6 per cent of the population. For our part we are convinced that any solution involving a radical division of the Punjab and Bengal, as would happen in this case, would be quite contrary to the wishes and interests of a large section of the population of these provinces. Bengal and Punjab both have their own common language and a long history and tradition. Moreover any division of Punjab would necessarily divide the racial territory of the Sikhs and leave substantial numbers of Sikhs on both sides of the frontier. We are therefore forced to the conclusion that neither a larger nor a smaller sovereign state of Pakistan would provide any acceptable solution of the internal problem. . . .'

Great Britain had never thought of shattering the unity of India of its own accord. The division was a programme of the Moslem League. The Attlee Government in Britain made every effort at that time to bring Moslems and Hindus together again, especially at the London conference in December 1946. There Great Britain went so far as to declare that she would recognize no Indian constitution which had not defined the mutual rights of Moslems and Hindus. However, the Moslem opposition was too strong, and in February 1947 the British Government proclaimed that in June it would hand over sovereign rights to 'one or two successor states', 'whereby it remains for the Indians themselves to decide whether the land is to be divided or not'.

The division of India has its historically conditioned causes. To attribute it to the British reveals unhistorical thinking or malice. When the British Parliament passed the law on Indian independence on 18th July 1947, *Dawn*, the official organ of the Moslem League, wrote that for this measure England 'deserved the highest praise from all freedom-loving peoples'. And the *Hindustan Times*, which supported the Congress Party, called it the noblest and most significant law ever proclaimed by the British Parliament. Also, if historical facts were different, one of the two partners would probably no longer be a member state of the Commonwealth.

All the more surprising is the interpretation which the Russians gave to the events leading finally to 15th August 1947, when the Union of India and Pakistan became independent and sovereign states. During his visit to Kashmir, Nikita Khrushchev caused surprise by a statement dealing with these events in which he said, amongst other things:

When India was freed from the yoke of colonialism, the Imperialists succeeded in dividing the country between India and Pakistan. This division was not made in the interests of the people but because of certain religious differences; no separation of that kind had anyway existed previously. In fact, the religious differences were not in truth the real reason for the division of India. Behind it stood a third power whose principle is, 'Divide and rule!' and this power used the religious differences for its own purposes.

The struggle for Pakistan was led by a generation of politicians educated in the West. For this reason some members of the strictly orthodox circles had regarded the creation of the future state with mistrust. Amongst these was such a man as the leader of the Jama'at-i-Islami movement, Syed Abul 'Ala Maudoodie. He eloquently expressed all his mistrust even in 1955 in his book *Islamic Law and Constitution*, which appeared in Karachi. A

similar struggle between orthodoxy and the West was at one time
a stirring intermezzo of nineteenth-century Russia, and had its
influence in the internal arrangements of the Jews for the future
state of Israel. This struggle is in abeyance in Israel only because
the Pan-Arab aspirations are seen as a common danger for the
state of Israel. In Pakistan the struggle between orthodoxy and
the West can still be traced as a theological and political dialogue.

The dynamic power of the first Pakistanis, of all the Iqbals,
Jinnahs, Liaquat Ali Khans and many others from the Moslem
League saw in Pakistan more than a territory of the old British
India, which had now received a special status. For them it was
the seed of a future empire of all Islam. And it was natural that
many people dreamed of the great caliphate embracing all Islamic
states. This was not so very strange, for the Moslems of the Indian
diaspora had been the most zealous supporters of the dignity of
the caliphate. When the Sultan was stripped of his temporal
power, the Indian Mohammedans set up the caliphate movement.
This movement also enjoyed the support of Hindu circles of the
Indian National Congress. And even when Ataturk ended the
caliphate in Turkey, the battle of the Indian supporters went on.
At that time some of them wanted to have the Nizam of Hyderabad proclaimed Caliph of all Islam. The heir to all these aspirations
was the state which was longed for by poets, philosophers and
politicians: Pakistan.

Today a reform movement, the Ahmadiyya, which goes back
to Hazrat Mirza Ghulam Ahmad (1835–1908), works for support
from Pakistan. The successor of this Ahmad called himself caliph.
Although this title was given up very quietly at his death, Ahmad's
followers have waited until the founder's son was old enough to
take over leadership of the movement. Today, from Rabwah in
Pakistan, Mirza Mahmud Ahmad seeks support as the 'second
caliph of the promised Messiah' and has organized the Ahmadiyya
into a powerful movement which conducts an Islamic mission in
many Western countries. *The Holy Qur-ân*, produced in Arabic
and in German, and published in 1954 in Hamburg and Zürich,
with a preface by the 'second caliph', is put into the hands of
Ahmadiyya missionaries in German-speaking countries.

As the Ahmadiyya does propaganda for a spiritual Pakistan,
without, however, identifying itself with the political Pakistan,
so is the land of Iqbal and Jinnah still the actual centre of a small

but energetic sect, or—according to the attitude of the individual Mohammedan to it—group within Islam: the Ismailites. This small community has won world-wide significance through the man who was at the same time its spiritual head and a politician, and who through his activity became one of the fathers of modern Pakistan: the Aga Khan. He had once played an important part in high diplomacy, as the first Moslem president of the League of Nations, and when he died on 11th January 1957, in his villa near Geneva, the Ismailites had become, financially, spiritually and socially, a leading community of Islam. The Aga Khan—that is only a title; his full name was His Highness Sir Sultan Mohammed Shah Aga Khan III—bequeathed his spiritual empire (which thanks to the willing sacrifice of twenty million financially sound supporters is also a reality) to his young grandson, the present Karim Aga Khan IV. The most magnificent of enthronements for the new Aga Khan took place on the soil of Pakistan. The Ismailites call the ceremony 'Takht Nashini', and more than eighty thousand people had hastened to be present at it in the National Stadium in Karachi. They made the 2nd Rajab 1377, that is 23rd January 1958, a day of national celebration for Pakistan. On this day Pakistan's leading newspaper *Dawn*, which had been founded by Mohammed Ali Jinnah in Delhi, gave a survey of the life of the last Ismaili Imam, who was simply the 'Aga Khan' to a whole generation; it described his Pan-Islamic position and his attitude to Pakistan:

In this connection it is interesting to point out that the Aga Khan foresaw a significant role for Pakistan and that he welcomed its birth because it would contribute to the greater honour of Islam. Not only did he praise the founding of Pakistan as 'the greatest success since the collapse of the caliphate', but he also stated: 'The period of the decline of Islam is over. Now Islam is in the ascendant once again. The future of Pakistan is bright.' And what is more, the Aga Khan saw in Pakistan a powerful instrument in the establishment of the world unity of Islam. He showed himself equally enthusiastic over the obligation which Pakistan had undertaken to build an Islamic state. After all, did not the venture of Pakistan fit into the framework of his own Pan-Islamism?

That the state of Pakistan pays so much attention to the small community of Shiite Ismailites is explained firstly by the outspoken politico-religious belief of the last Aga Khan, who was born in Karachi and therefore always looked upon it as his home;

it is also explained by the numerous connections of his Ismailite supporters with all parts of the earth and particularly with East Africa, the Near East, Burma, Iran and Central Asia. In northern Kashmir the Mir of Hunza is one of the best-known supporters of the Ismailite branch of Islam. From these circles attempts are made again and again to remove the division of Moslems into Sunnites and Shiites. However, Pakistan has been for a long time the ideal spiritual ground for the maturing of these ideas.

Administrators of modern states have not much time to devote to spiritual and religious meditation. In Pakistan, however, political problems must be considered in the light of the conflicting demands of the Eastern and Western Provinces of the state, while the government must carry on both by the printed and by the spoken word a bitter feud, on the one hand with its Afghan neighbours on the problem of Pakhtunistan, and on the other with India over Kashmir. The constitutional problem is still not solved, but the constitution which came into force on 23rd March 1956 was abolished on 7th October 1958, three weeks before General Ayub Khan seized power. But the new head of state believed it necessary to provide the country with a new symbol of its unity in the shape of a new capital, still to be built in the neighbourhood of Rawalpindi, a scheme first projected in August 1960, whereby the name of the new capital will probably be Islamabad. The new experiment of Pakistan under the name of basic democracy bears not so much the stamp of political boldness as of prudent marking time.

The dream of world supremacy, which was once dreamed on the banks of the Indus and found its interpretation in the Indian Moslem University of Aligarh, must today give way to cooler and more matter-of-fact considerations. Pan-Islam is inscribed on the banner of those people who wish first of all to see the political challenge of Pan-Arabism made a reality. The centre of its strength is the city of Al-Azhar University. And working from Cairo it temporarily drew the city of the Umayyads, Damascus, and that of the Abbasids, Bagdad, into its power. But from there the vibrations of political and religious spheres of influence can be felt as far away as the Indus.

There, however, the bold plans of the Islamic universe are being sorted out. It is necessary to scheme and to calculate: where is the water for the parched fields of West Pakistan to come from, how is the falling price of jute to be met or how is the internal tension between supporters of a federal state and those of a one-state system to be smoothed out? There are endless problems, simple, nerve-wracking problems of how to fill the people's food bowls. Daily life gazes into the ministerial offices with their bright-coloured pictures of the Quaid-i-Azam over there in Karachi, in Dacca, in Lahore. . . .

8

Drama in Kashmir

THE 'PEARL OF THE HIMALAYAS' BECOMES THE APPLE OF DISCORD OF A SUBCONTINENT

POETS and writers have praised the beauty of Kashmir. The green plains in the river valleys, the snow-covered mountain tops, the house-boats on the lakes, the powerful type of happy mountain people live on in the verses of the poets.

However, today it is not the poets but the politicians who are especially interested in Kashmir. Those twin children of the Union of India and Pakistan, born in the middle of August 1947, have since the partition fought bitterly for this beautiful spot in the Himalayan foothills.

The problem of Kashmir has been ever present in the history of modern India. In 1932 Iqbal wrote in his *Javid Nameh*, already mentioned on page 72: 'In the people of Kashmir the soul burns like straw; and cries of pain burst from their throat.'

The problem of this state arose from its political situation. A Hindu ruler, a Maharajah, ruled over a people consisting mainly of Moslems. In the old India Kashmir was the counterpart of the state of Hyderabad, where the situation was exactly the opposite: the Mohammedan Nizam ruled over subjects who were mainly Hindus.

Kashmir is the dreamland of the Indian subcontinent. It is so to such an extent that even plain statesmen seize their pens to

82

sing the praise of this country. Since the emperor Jehangir surrendered in 1620 to the spell of Kashmir, there followed many others whose pens were dedicated only to political matters. Finally, one of the most famous statesmen of our time, Jawaharlal Nehru, has praised the beauty of Kashmir in his book entitled 'The Discovery of India'. Nehru himself is descended from a race of Kashmir Brahmins. Let me mention another statesman from Soviet territory: the present president of Uzbekistan, Sharof Rashidov, published in 1957 in Tashkent a small Uzbek volume, *Kashmir Koshigy*, that is, 'Song of Kashmir'. An Uzbek guide told me that the book is supposed to have arisen solely from a poet's inspiration and to contain no political undertones.

The word 'Kashmir', which is used generally for the strips of land between the River Jhelum and the Karakorum Pass over which Pakistan and the Union of India are in dispute, is not quite correct. *Kashmir* is actually only the vale of Kashmir—that is, the city of Srinagar and district. In addition, however, there is Jammu, a region which runs right into the plains of the 'five river country' and whose namesake capital served as a winter residence for the Maharajahs of Kashmir. Another region is Ladakh, a large country but sparsely populated, whose inhabitants are for the most part lamaistic Buddhists. Formerly—until 1837—Ladakh was also politically a part of the Dalai Lama's state, as was also the most northerly part of greater Kashmir, Baltistan, which was added to Kashmir in 1839. Finally, Gilgit belonged nominally to Kashmir. However, the links joining this territory to Srinagar were very tenuous, and in 1889 the British created out of the strategically very important but very thinly populated region the so-called Gilgit Agency under a British Agent. The pressure of Russia was at that time very noticeable in the Pamir area.

Kashmir's history is gay and colourful like its nature. Kalhana was the first of its numerous chroniclers. His early medieval work on the history of this country, so often celebrated as the 'pearl of the Himalayas', is a recitation of the deeds of the Kashmiri rulers. He called it *Rajtarangni*, that is, 'River of the Kings'. This river, on which the boats of the dynasties sail with gleaming colours, begins—how could it be otherwise?—in mythical times. But when it enters the historical landscape, the memory of the myth is forgotten. Then one notices that Kalhana was one of the first Indians who strove to be an exact chronicler and historian.

The succession of rulers leads from the mythical king Gonanda I, by way of all the Hindu and Buddhist bearers of proud names from the Kashmiri, Indian, Scythian and Kushanian races, to the princes of the Islamic faith who made a home for the *armagan-i Hidjaz*, the present of the Hidjas, the religion of Mohammed, in the mountains of Kashmir.

The first to accept Islam was a Tibetan prince who lived at the court of the ruler of Kashmir, Simha Dev. He was called Renchen Shah and for a short time (1325–7) ascended the throne of Kashmir, after marrying a royal princess. But when the Brahmins, led by one of their members, Devaswami, refused to receive the Tibetan prince into one of their high Hindu castes (which in the opinion of the Hindus was also impossible), Renchen swore an oath that he would take the faith of the first man he met on the following morning. The next morning he saw an Islamic pilgrim, Bulbul Shah, whose faith he adopted, and he assumed the title Sadar ud-Din. That was three years after an attack by the descendant of Genghis Khan, Zulfi Kadir Khan, upon Kashmir, in which thousands of Brahmins perished and thus for the first time felt the effects of fanaticism. In the fifteenth century one of the Moslem princes, Sikandar, bore the name of 'image breaker'. At that time the Hindu temples were converted into mosques or transformed into a desolate heap of ruins. The Buddhist temple of Parihasapura and the Hindu Sun Temple of Martand recall even today in outline and ruins a memory of their former greatness. Another of the temple ruins, a place for historical meditation, is Aba Van, once the meeting-place of the snake worshippers of Kashmir. Indian mythology tells of the human snake race of the Nagas. It traces its descent from the wise man Kasyapa who once married two women, the eldest of whom, Kudru, became the mother of these creatures, half man, half snake. Many Hindu scholars see in snake worship one of the original forms of religious life. In this connection they draw particular attention to the Egypt of the Pharaohs and to Aztec sanctuaries in Tenochtitlan, Mexico. They even draw parallels with the Bible and see in these Nagas (not of course to be confused with the tribe in Assam) the original model of the snake which was once able to beguile Eve in Paradise. But they forget that this biblical snake has more of a symbolic content and that the Hebrew interpretation is a different one from that of the Hindus, whose Nagas belong to the Hindu jungle of mythology.

The Mohammedan dynasties in Kashmir, who allowed in turn Kashmiris, Chaks, Moghuls and Afghans to replace each other, ruled until 1819. In that year the rulers of the Punjab, the Sikhs, interfered in the internal disturbances which had broken out in the last years during the Afghan dominion in Kashmir, and until 1846 they sent their governors to Srinagar.

Jammu was at that time not yet joined to Kashmir, and one of its Sikh governors had been Gulab Singh, who had in 1841 allowed the British to cross Jammu in order to march against the Afghans. The long-standing battle of the lords of Kabul allowed Gulab Singh to be quickly placed on the British map, whilst the court in Lahore was still hesitating. However, it was not long before the British had made the Sikhs themselves into enemies. Once again it was Gulab Singh who smoothed things out, and as a friend of Britain sought to mediate. When the first war with the Sikhs ended in a victory for the British, the ruler of the Punjab found himself obliged to grant him complete independence. Nevertheless Gulab Singh had to pay the British 75 lakhs of rupees for it (one lakh is 100,000 rupees), whereby the court of Lahore could make reparation for the war debts for the lost war. All the same Lahore was to pay £1,500,000 sterling. But thus was found—irony of world history—in the friend of Britain, Gulab Singh, the man who to be sure became independent, but had to put the seal to his friendship in a somewhat remarkable manner. In the Treaty of Lahore, concluded with Gulab Singh and signed on the 9th March 1846, is the statement:

In recognition of the services which the Rajah Gulab Singh of Jammu rendered to the State of Lahore by working for the reopening of friendly relations between Lahore and the British Government, the Maharajah Dhuleep Singh herewith recognizes the independent sovereign rule of the Rajah Gulab Singh in the territories and mountain regions which are handed over to the said Rajah Gulab Singh by a special agreement between him and the British Government. Also included are the dependent regions which have been in the possession of the Rajah since the time of the Maharajah Kharak Singh, and the British Government promises, in recognition of the good behaviour of the Rajah Gulab Singh, to recognize his independence in these territories and to grant him the privilege of a special peace with the British Government.

Exactly seven days later, on 16th March 1846, Rajah Gulab Singh signed the Peace of Amritsar. The Rajah emerged from it as Maharajah of Jammu and Kashmir. These new lords of Kashmir belonging to a new caste, that of 'H. H.' (His Highness), were, along with four other royal rulers, amongst the 584 more or less powerful Indian princes existing in 1947, to be entitled to a twenty-one-gun salute as sovereign kings.

In Amritsar, Gulab Singh, who had in any case long since broken with the Sikh community, had undertaken (Article 3) to pay 71 million rupees (Nanakshahi), had recognized the British Government as arbiter in foreign affairs (Article 5), and had declared that he would never appoint European or American officials without the express permission of the British Government (Article 7). But, as a small visible sign of British suzerainty, the Maharajah of Kashmir had to bear the 'sacrifice' contained in Article 10:

Maharajah Gulab Singh recognizes the suzerainty of the British Government and, as a sign of the recognition of this suzerainty, will hand over as a gift each year to the British Government a horse, twelve goats (six male and six female) and three pairs of Kashmir shawls.

By the Amritsar Treaty the region which is today so strongly contested was made over to the race of Gulab Singh, to the dynasty of the Dogra 'for perpetual, independent possession'. The 'sale of Kashmir' has always been a subject in the internal history of India and Kashmir over which opposing sides were to become inflamed. But it was the beginning of a new epoch in which the people gradually discovered that they are not only an object. Yet it has been a long time in Asia until those who were the object are also the subject.

The first sign of a stirring of the will of the people can be discovered in about 1927, when leaflets were distributed in which the Government of the Dogra country was challenged to make it possible not only for Hindus and Sikhs but also for the majority of the country, the Moslems, to take up state appointments. In 1930 groups of the so-called 'Reading Room Party' were formed under the Moslem Youth. Here it was a question of groups possessing only a loose connection with each other through a common view of life, but a real organization was still lacking. The Maharajah replied to the challenge in 1931 by allowing three parties to canvass for members. These were the Kashmiri Pandits' conference, the Hindu Saba in Jammu, and the Sikhs' Shiromani Khalsa Darbar. As can be guessed from the proper nouns, it was only a question of non-Moslem groups. The resistance of the Moslems was especially fired by a young teacher, the son of a shawl dealer, who had studied in Lahore and Aligarh: Sheik Mohammed Abdullah. With this there appeared for the first time upon the political stage of Kashmir the man who, after the great revolt of 1931, was named *Sher-e-Kashmir* (the 'Lion of Kashmir'). Abdullah had to go to prison for some months. In October 1932 he founded the All-Jammu and Kashmir Muslim Conference. The attacks which were made from the Mohammedan side of Kashmir upon the Dogra Government disturbed and alarmed even London. The first Kashmir commission, the so-called Glancy Commission, was sent to Srinagar to investigate the troubles and to recommend urgent reforms to the Maharajah.

The struggle of the Muslim Conference against the Maharajah was, according to the wish of Sheik Abdullah, to see Hindus and Sikhs also as partners of the Islamic population. Therefore in 1935 he founded the weekly paper *Hamdard* with the Kashmir Brahmin Prem Nath Bazaz. However, the leadership of the Muslim Conference did not identify itself with the opinion of its founder. In the ideas of the Indian National Congress Abdullah found the conceptions which were to become the programme of a new group. In 1939 Sheik Abdullah abruptly broke away from his own creation, the Muslim Conference, and announced the foundation of the All-Jammu and Kashmir National Conference. The first president of this union was to be Ghulam Mohammed Sadiq, who is, however, today the advocate in Kashmir of the Communist Party of India.

The Moslem population, together with Hindus and Sikhs, went over to Abdullah. His name worked like a magnet. Nevertheless, since Jinnah had visited Kashmir in 1943, the breach which ran through the whole of India could be traced in Kashmir too. The struggle against the Maharajah, which so far had united the Kashmiris, suddenly put before the Moslems of Kashmir the question which faced all Indian Mohammedans: For or against Pakistan?

Once again the hostile groups amongst the Moslems came together after the Maharajah had thrown the leaders of both

G

groups into prison. The time of negotiations began when Great Britain declared herself prepared to give the Indians their freedom.

And history opens up stirring years in the story of modern Kashmir: Abdullah becomes Prime Minister, Pakistani tribes penetrate as far as Kashmir, India is asked for support, the United Nations are alerted. And finally the famous Cease Fire Line, the demarcation line between the Pakistani and Indian part of the country, divides the land. Battles for the land are taken before the forum of the United Nations. At last we see the vision of a self-sufficient Kashmir. Abdullah's dreams end in prison. Then we hear of the dramatic release and re-arrest of the 'Lion'.

Kashmir lies like an angle, like a pillar holding West Pakistan and India together. Yet exactly the opposite is the case. The land which could inspire poets could not use its strength to unite the two enemy brothers of the greater Bharat Mata. Kashmir is the sore spot burning in the midst of the Union of India and Pakistan.

For the Union of India it is a question of the principle of her statesmanship: that India is only one, that the unity of the country is shown in its diversity, that all Hindus, Moslems, Sikhs, Jains, Jews and Christians are children of one and the same earth. For Pakistan other things are at stake in Kashmir: that Hindus and Moslems form two different spheres of life, which could not be united in their views on religion, Ahimsa philosophy, caste, the position of women and in other problems.

Perhaps the greatest contrast in the question of one nation or two nations lies in the simple acceptance of the conception of nationhood. In the old Osman empire the name 'nation' was given to individual religious communities. They were called 'millet', but this conception is somewhat different from the European 'nation'. It is not the first time in modern history that Western ideas on the philosophy of the state are clashing so vehemently with Islamic ones. A similar tension between Western ideas on the state and Islamic views was found in Sicily in the time of the Hohenstaufen. One hundred and fifty years later, when the Hohenstaufen dreams of world dominion had faded, Ibn Khaldun wrote his *Muqadima*, his ideas upon the state, upon the soil of Africa where once Augustine had thought out his *Civitas Dei*. The central idea of the former is the *asabijja*, which describes feeling for race, love of home, sense of community and similar feelings. Here lies the seed of the Islamic nation. It is exactly the *natio* in the medieval sense, in which the guilds of university students were also called 'nations'. Nevertheless Ibn Khaldun, too, plays an important part in the philosophical struggle for Pakistan. 'The universal states which have a widespread sphere of government, arise from religion either on the basis of a prophecy or a sermon,' is written in the *Muqadima*. Ibn Khaldun's reflections on the medieval state are still influential amongst Moslems today. Historical research calls him a realistic historical thinker. The reality of Pakistan, which in any case includes the problem of Kashmir, has justified him in modern times.

However, these are philosophical meditations on the state. For years the reality of Kashmir has been preoccupying world public opinion. Two plans for its solution may be named, in order to show how thinking in Asiatic circles can swing, at once iridescent and dynamic, between the extreme opposites of Utopia and reality. The plan of the Utopians: create in a world federation the Aryan Region, including Iran and India and the neighbouring countries! Thus speaks Aryan Peshwa Mahendra Pratap Raja, demanding that Srinagar in Kashmir shall be proclaimed the capital of this region (Honolulu is to be the world capital). The journal of *Aryan Peshwa* ('World Federation') bears the following sub-heading: 'Started at Berlin in September 1929, a few numbers published from U.S.A. From November 1930 to March 1942 published in Japan and China, but mostly in Japan. Now regularly appearing in India, every month, since November 1946.' And by way of contrast a realistic plan. The *Hindustan Standard* announced in a report from Cuttack on 16th February 1958:

Sri H. V. Kamath, the leader of the Praja Socialists, declared here that the final solution of Indo-Pakistani relations will be a kind of reunion. He did not know how long it would be necessary to wait, but for the next ten or twenty years he foretold some kind of a federation between India and Pakistan. . . .

Kashmir is so far away; and yet a bit of this Kashmir has always been with us. The 'Pearl of the Himalayas' is in fact the original home of the gipsies. They once came in the train of the great Mongol invasion of Europe. These small Indoeuropean races in caravans, whose tribal kings preserve ancient nomad customs right down to our days, have in some regions of Germany been called Tartars, recalling the race of conquerors whom they followed. For seven hundred years they brought a breath of the romance of the nomad to the West and told of their home in the Himalayas which has not until modern times been opened up to public consciousness. However, at present this consciousness is awakening with a drama which has, generally speaking, become a sign of modern political development, allowing no time to devote one's thoughts to a romantic intermezzo of restless wandering between peoples and continents.

Theme Song Neutrality

AFGHANISTAN TAKES SWITZERLAND
AS A MODEL

In February 1958, when Mohammed Zahir Shah Almottawakal Alallah, the King of the Afghans, was on a state visit in the Indian capital, New Delhi, having travelled there from Karachi, a song of welcome written in Gurmurkhi was distributed. This song, in the language of the Punjab and the writing of the Sikhs, was composed by 'Prabhjot', an authoress who is a legend in the literary world of the Punjabi-speaking Indians (Sardarni Prabhjot Kaur is the wife of the then Indian military attaché in Kabul, Major N. P. Singh). The end of the song was as follows:

> . . . Rang vatayā jag nē lok barē balvān
> Mahan dip hai Asia dil vangu Afghān
> Dhan hai tērē dēsh tta sohne purakh-Māhān
> Gagno vadi ātmā jigrā vāng Chitān.
> Ji āyān hāmsaio āvo khēran nal
> Ral rachāvān gē asi ik sunēhra kal.

> . . . The world has changed and the people became strong.
> Asia is a great continent and Afghanistan is like its heart.
> The wealth of your country—that is your brave people—
> Great of soul and with courage strong as rocks.
> Welcome, dear neighbours, welcome!
> Together we will build the future—peaceful and golden!

'. . . and Afghanistan is like its heart' wrote this woman from the Punjab. Twenty-five years earlier her fellow countryman

91

Iqbal had dedicated similar verses to this land of Afghanistan lying in the heart of the continent of Asia:

> If the heart dies, the body is nothing: nothing at all.
> Look to the heart, otherwise bind yourself to nothing.
> This Asia is a form made of clay and water;
> Afghanistan is the heart of this being—
> If it dies, Asia will perish,
> If it flourishes, Asia will recover.

These lines of Iqbal have always reminded me of similar words, more universally applied, which a Finn once wrote about Germany. He was Veikko Antero Koskenniemi, who after the First World War wrote the warning message that Germany's evening was the evening of the world, and Germany's morning the morning of the world.

But Afghanistan too can be considered more universally. It is not only the geographical heart. It is the cornerstone of that great empire of the spirit which shone forth from Hellas and from here found, artistically and intellectually, a wonderful synthesis between East and West. The spirit of Greece reached as far as here. It also reached Turkestan, but its impetus perished on the Tibetan-Mongolian wastelands. And so it did not embrace the world of China and did not venture to make the leap into the truly universal. What Hellenism could not reach has been reached by the culture formed in the country later known as Afghanistan. Buddhist art bearing a Graeco-Bactrian imprint has fertilized the creative will of artists far into the Sino-Asiatic intellectual field.

Afghanistan formed the synthesis of this Bactrian art which shone out directly towards the east. But at the same time the country lies on that frontier region where different religious worlds clash. The belief in God Almighty as monotheists see it, which was developed particularly amongst the Semitic, Turanian and Indoeuropean tribes, reached to the very foothills of the Himalayas. The desert and the steppe strengthened still more this monotheistic faith, which from time immemorial lies like a priceless gift in the heart of humanity. But beyond the Indus there lay, extreme like the tropics, the very different realm of polytheism, which by its preference for one divinity above all others, by henotheism, returned to the road to monotheism, and found it also in individual Hindu philosophies. China's religious world, on the basis of an ancient cult of ancestors and of heaven, opened up new spiritual horizons, where philosophy shone brighter than religion, and where the godhead was replaced by *Tao*, an energy and substance guiding world events. Buddha's ungodly message also flowed into it all. And to the faith of the great mass of people who united the world of god, Taoism and Buddha, was added the official religion of Confucianism, an example of the separation between official religious form and popular faith which is so frequent in Far Eastern culture. And finally Afghanistan looks towards Tibet which, with Mongolian territory, forms the lamaistic Buddhist island in the midst of Asia and adds remarkable colour to the religious map of the world.

From Balkh in present-day Afghanistan went forth that dynamic strength which has already been mentioned, which embraced the Hellenistic and East Iranian cultures and made the area of the western Himalayas a unique cultural centre. Proceeding from this, streams of new impulses and of artistic and intellectual visions seized the peoples of the south-east Asian and Far Eastern countries.

Different and often contradictory elements have come together in the cultural world of Balkh (formerly called Bactria). Therefore it is a difficult undertaking to indicate the essence and the growth of this cultural epoch. Formerly the intellectual world of what was later Afghanistan was completely determined by the Aryan world of the lords of this country. It was the culture of a race of knights and horsemen. Its intellectual and religious world may have been that of the so-called Kafir in Hindu Kush, in the most eastern part of Afghanistan.

In that country called Nuristan, but generally known as Kafiristan, there lived tribes who maintained their old customs right into the nineteenth century. Also their conception of religion dated from the pre-Islamic and Buddhist time. The Kafir were of the opinion that gods were like diamonds. They said *Imra Suntarna* and with these words expressed the essence of the divine. Amongst their neighbours these Kafir (the word means 'unbelievers') bore the name *Sia-Posh*, which can be translated as something like 'dressed in black'. The highest goddess was generally called *Kumay*. The name of a wise man *Gish*, who appears again and again in the stories of the Kafir tribes, tells of contact with Islam. Amongst other names he was also called

Akaksn Manugish or *Abujal*. In the latter, however, one can trace Abu Kakam Ben Hashem ben Moghayera, one of the eminent Meccans of the time of Mohammed, who was among the bitterest enemies of the prophet. Other gods of the Kafir tribes were the god of causation, *Moan*; *Baghisht*, the giver of nourishment; and the protector of homes, *Salmuch*. The number of gods of the old Kafiri could mean that we were concerned here with a polytheistic faith. These gods were mostly tribal gods which bore different names, but in spite of their special power to give nourishment or protect homes, they were always regarded as the 'god'. Thus the people of Wama formerly called their god *Indra*, the Shopo gave him the name *Mara* and the Arnsi, *Imra*. In other tribes the creator of the world was called *Pashashay*. The festivals of the people of Kafiristan were determined by the rhythm of the year, which was reflected in the meetings of the peasants. Thus, for example, in the month *Nilo*, which announced the beginning of spring, when herds were driven out of the stalls and into the green pastures, the small tribe of the Shopo sang the *Disaninat*, the song to *Disani*, the heavenly watchman, who among the eighteen duties prescribed for him had, among other things, to see to the well-being of cows, shepherds, children, and the protection of the village organization.

Then there penetrated into this peasant world the message of Zarathustra, which was appearing for the first time in the East Iranian and Bactrian region. The world of this prophet is often linked with Platonic ideas, or again by others with the Aristotelean structure of thought. In the Hellenic world Zarathustra was known as Zoroaster, and his world is quite different from that of the racially related Aryan Indians. Zarathustra represented a monotheistic conception—at least with one modification. His god is a supreme god, *Ahura Mazda*. It is he who reigns, yet at the same time another rules with him: *Ahriman*, the principle of evil. Ahura Mazda is the Eternal, the High, the Wise One, the Creator and Final Judge. But at the same time, from all eternity, Ahriman was given with him to the world. Perhaps the dualistic principle, which is nevertheless built upon monotheism, is the inheritance of a primeval myth of divine twins. However, the dualistic conception of the world was embodied in this myth. The deep preoccupation with eschatological matters gave to the prophet of Ahura Mazda, whose teaching is preserved in the sacred book of the *Avesta*, the certainty that one day his supreme god would overcome the demon of evil. In the victory of the good, in the optimistic faith in the future rule of the truth, is shown the genuinely monotheistic character of the Zarathustrian faith which is today called the Parsee religion.

In this world man has of his own free will to decide for Ahura Mazda or for Ahriman. The lofty ethical conception in this faith, in which personal, moral, free responsibility has to guide man, is still prevalent today amongst the last adherents of the prophet Zarathustra, who live in peasant settlements in East Iran, and from the urban, highly civilized world of Bombay has spread over the most important commercial cities of the Indian sub-continent. The Parsees—this word means Persians—still preserve an ancient Aryan fire cult. For them death is something impure. But especially it was impossible for them to burn the dead with holy fire, as the Hindus did. In the same way it was originally unthinkable for the followers of Zarathustra to bury the corpses in the earth. Therefore they gave the dead to the vultures. Near Bombay, which shelters the largest Parsee colony in the world, stand therefore the towers of silence (*dakhma*) proclaiming what to us seems to be a lack of respect for the dead. But in reality it is perhaps something quite different: the seeming lack of respect shows how greatly the Parsee is influenced by eschatological thought. He sees fulfilment only on the other side. The earthly life is only a reflection of the real life. And why should one show any kind of respect for the mirror, the earthly body, when the person who is reflected in it now sees the other, the real life?

The highest symbol for the followers of Zarathustra is fire—that which burns in the temples and that of the sun—and when they pray they gaze towards these lights. This has often led to the belief that the Zoroastrians, as they are often also called, are fire worshippers. But the reason for the loving care of the fire ritual is only to represent the purity of God in the pure fire and so as to be able to attain for themselves *vohu mano* ('pure thinking'). In ancient Iran three principal fires used to burn—one, *Adhur Farnbag*, the fire of Khvarnah on the mountain of Khvarrehomand, was the sanctuary of the priests. *Adhur Gushnasp* on Mount Asnavand burned as the warriors' fire, whilst *Adhur Burzin Mihr*, the fire of high Mithra on Mount Rewand, was intended for the rank of peasants. *Atar* (fire) still burns today in a few small spiritual oases of Parseedom and recalls the East Iranian Bactrian home of the Zarathustrian religion, where long ago the holy light was called *puthro Ahurahe Mazdao* ('child of Ahura Mazda'), and shone forth as a belief in Almighty God into the Aryan world, becoming an official acknowledgment of the great Persian Empire.

Then the conqueror appeared from Macedonia. From the old trading centre, Balkh, grew the Greek Bactria, the capital of the *choora Bactria* or of the Bactrian landscape. On the spot where caravans from China, Central Asia, India and Iran met and offered their wares, from silk to opium, an Indianized Little Hellas was built up, handing on by way of the trade routes into neighbouring countries its ideas and artistic ornaments and sculpture. The fresh air of the Afghan mountains worked wonders when the Hellenistic shapes and art forms appeared up here in the midst of the Asiatic continent. Arnold Toynbee speaks of the subject in his book, *Civilization on Trial*:

As the Greek art of the 'Hellenistic' and the early 'Imperial' age spreads eastward, across the dead body of the defunct Persian Empire, until it reaches Afghanistan, it becomes more and more conventional and commercial and lifeless. And then something like a miracle happens. This fast degenerating Greek art collides in Afghanistan with another spiritual force which is radiating out of India: the Mahayana form of Buddhism. And the degenerating Greek art unites with the Mahayana to form a distinctively new and intensely creative civilization: the Mahayanian Buddhist civilization which has travelled north-eastward across Asia to become the civilization of the Far East.

This new world was the *imperium* of Gandara art. Its body was Greek and was born on the shores of the Aegean. But its spirit was Indian, springing from the world of the Ganges, which rises in the Himalayas. This Bactrian culture reached a peak in the Indoeuropean Kushan empire of King Kanishka in the second century A.D. There began then the Indianization of art which found its highest expression later under the Gupta rulers.

But in this way Hellenism tilled the cultural soil of India. From the Macedonian Alexander had developed in the popular legend the Iranianized relation of Darius, who fought with the ruler of Iran for the crown. It was an especial event which had formerly linked Alexander with the country which was to preserve longest the name of Greece in Central Asia. It was in fact a Bactrian princess, Rushang-Roxane, who became Alexander's wife and whose marriage became the symbol of that east-west synthesis which the great Macedonian had so deeply wished.

And in the footsteps of the Hellenes wandered later the men who bore in their hearts the belief in Mithras. They were followed by the first Nestorian Christians. Nestorianism held for many years the position of an Iranian imperial church. It flourished alongside the communities of the Zarathustrian religion. They were not in fact—in the fourth and later centuries—the first Christians to touch the fringe of the Himalayas. Legend has it that already in the first half of the first century, under the Saka ruler Gondophares, who was called *Vindafarna* in the Iranian language, the apostle St Thomas did missionary work in the Bactrian-North Indian part of this region. St Thomas may be a legend here, but in the South Indian region of the Malayalees and Tamils his influence is without doubt an historical fact.

In the seventh century, when Mohammed proclaimed from the holy places of Hedjaz his gospel of devotion to God, to Islam, the dynamic power of the new religion was expressed also by military organization. And the preachers of the new doctrine knocked at the gates of Bactria too, and the armies came, wanting to create by force the Islamic kingdom upon earth.

As Balkh once shone in the Graeco-Bactrian Indian epoch, so in the early Islamic period the fame of being the capital of the Afghan region fell to Ghazni. And with the prophets of Islam Afghanistan made the acquaintance of the great Macedonian for the second time, only he was wrapped in an oriental garment. Alexander had become *Dhu L'Karnain*—that is to say, the 'two-horned one'. The horns, which had formerly been an attribute of Jupiter Ammon in the land of Egypt, now belonged to Iskander the hero, who was to survive in the sagas and legends of three continents. Even in the *Koran*, the sacred book of Islam, there is talk of this 'two-horned one'. Thus it is written in the Sura Al-Kahf (xviii. 93–8):

Hereupon he followed a (different) way until he arrived between the two mountains and at their foot found a people who could scarcely understand a word.

They spoke: 'O Dhu L'Karnain, truly Gog and Magog cause disorder upon earth; may we now pay tribute to you on condition that you erect a barrier between us and them?'

He answered: 'The power with which my lord has equipped me for that purpose is better, yet you may lend me your arm and I will erect a strong barrier between you and them. Bring me pieces of iron!'

They did so until he had levelled the space between the two mountain slopes, and said: 'Blow with your bellows!' They blew until he had finished and said: 'Bring me molten copper, that I may pour it over!'

Thus they [Gog and Magog] could not climb over the barrier, nor could they make holes through it.

That event, describing the conquest of a mountainous country, with which the Old Testament names of Gog and Magog are linked, is in the opinion of many interpreters of the Koran connected with the region of the Himalayas, into which the Macedonian armies once penetrated. Perhaps the world of the Himalayan mountains, whose reputation for wild, impassable ravines had reached as far as Israel, was the original model for Gog and Magog, where land and ruler of the unbelievers are already symbolized in wild nature.

In the eleventh century Ghazni became the capital of an empire in which a Turkish ruling class made Islam the state religion. Individual Turks had already for long penetrated as far as Bagdad and earned their bread as mercenaries at the courts of the caliphs. Just as formerly the praetorians of Germanic origin dedicated themselves to the service of Imperial Rome, and individuals amongst them wielded great power as military commanders and governors, so it was with the Turks and their first relationship to the Arab rulers.

The first Turk, with his 'people of twice a hundred thousand tents', to accept Islam and thus pave the way for the entry of the Turks into the Islamic world state was, in the area of present-day West Turkestan, the western Qarachanid Qarluq ruler Satuk Bughra Khan (A.D. 955). This ruler made North Turkestan Moslem; in the east and west of the country the religion of the prophet Mohammed was accepted. The followers of the prophet sent their military missionaries even into the Tarim basin. But in the south of Turkestan another Turk was fortunate enough to establish himself as ruler. He was Mohammed (or Mahmud) of Ghazni, named thus after his subsequent capital on Afghan soil. This Turkish ruler of ancient Bactria gazed from the mountains under his control down on to the Indian plains. He undertook seventeen campaigns, brought back rich spoils and wanted to carry the faith of the prophet into the land of the Hindus. With his victory over the Rajah Jaipal of the Hindu Shahiyya dynasty, in 1001, Mohammed of Ghazni showed the sons of Afghanistan the way to India. A century and a half later the conqueror of northwest India is called Mohammed of Ghor; and not much later there came the establishment of the sultanate of Delhi (1206–1526). Again and again Afghans form the backbone of Islamic missions and Mohammedan conquest in northern India.

In the fifteenth century Herat became a centre of Timurid rule. In the sixteenth, members of the old Turkish family set out from here to gain possession of India. The imperial power of the Moghuls was founded by the same means which Mohammed of Ghazni had once wanted to employ in conquering the Indian countryside. While they were building up their power in India, Afghanistan fell a prey to the Persians, who, under the Safiwids, were occupying the western part of the country, whilst the eastern part later fell again to the Moghuls. This state of affairs lasted until the beginning of the eighteenth century.

In 1709 the Afghan commandant of the town of Kalantar rose against the Persian governor of Kandahar. The rebel against the imperial power of Iran was Mir Wais Khan. He belonged to the race of the Hotaki and was to set in motion the movement for self-determination of modern Afghanistan. Similarly, the Abdali of Herat rose up, and even carried the Afghan attack into the very heart of Persia. However, the Persian reaction was soon to begin under Nadir Kuli Khan, who in 1730 had ended the Afghan threat to Persia. As Nadir Shah, he carried on the attack not only against Afghanistan, but also penetrated far into the kingdom of the Great Moghuls. In 1739 he brought the peacock throne from Delhi to Persia, and from then on it was to become the symbol of imperial Persia-Iran. Yet when in 1740 Nadir Shah was murdered in his bivouac of Kabushan, the old Persian dream of an Asiatic world empire reaching from Anatolia to the plains of India was destined to become reality only for a short time, and then to fade away completely. But instead of political rule, the victorious compaign of the Persian language was to be renewed. The saying was already current amongst Moslems that faith belonged to the Arabs, art to the Persians and government to the Turks. The saying from the Islamic had a parallel in that Christian medieval trinity: the *sacerdotium* belongs to Italy, *studium* to France and *imperium* to Germany.

A new star appeared on the horizon of Islamic powers: Ahmed Khan Abdali, from the branch of the family calling itself *Dur-i Durran* ('peal of time'), whence the family later adopted the general name of Durrani. In October 1747, when Nadir Shah had been killed, the Afghans held a tribal assembly, a *jirga*, in Kandahar. They wanted to choose their own ruler. When they could not agree a holy dervish made the decision by boldly placing the crown upon the head of a young Afghan leader. But the crown, a symbol of the peasant nobility of these mountain races, was made of whatever gifts of God the fields could offer. An Afghan historian, Ahmad Ali Kohzad, wrote of it in a brochure (No. 44 of the Historical Society of Afghanistan), *Men and Events through Eighteenth and Nineteenth Century Afghanistan*:

In the year 1160 after the Hejira (flight of Mohammed from Mecca to Medina), that is in A.D. 1782, a royal coronation took place in the sanctuary of Shair Surkh in Kandahar. There was a similar coronation in Kabul Siah-Sung in the year 1254 after the Hejira, that is, in A.D. 1876. Both coronations were simple ceremonies to mark the ascent to the throne of Afghan kings. A crown of rye was set upon the head of one of them, and upon the head of the other a crown of wheat. It was the great dervish, Sabir Shah, a well-known Sufi prophet, who performed the ceremony in Kandahar, and in Kabul it was Mir Hajjhi, son of Mir Wayaz. But the men who wore these crowns of wheat and rye were Ahmed Shah Durrani, founder of the royal Durrani dynasty, and Emir Doust, the first of the royal house of Mohammadzai.

The history of the eighteenth and nineteenth centuries, as regards Afghanistan and India, was once again an exchange between Afghans and British. The plains of the Indus and Ganges valleys had always attracted the men of Afghanistan. But the answer came from the British, who, as Russia's pressure grew nearer and nearer to the Pamir mountains, tried to conquer the land of the Afghans. The British also incited the Persians to resume possession of the western part of the Afghan provinces. In this situation Shah Shuja became a victim of the confusion of the times. He had to leave his country, and went to Lahore to the court of the Sikhs. Here he left in the hands of his hosts a valuable present, the Koh-i-Noor diamond, which was later to become part of the British crown jewels. In 1838 it was in fact possible for the British to intervene in the question of the Afghan succession, which started the first Afghan-British war. But after a brief royal intermezzo, during which Shah Shuja, with British help, once more ascended the throne, it ended with a painful shock to the British. The Afghans under Dost Mohammed Khan were finally successful and compelled the British on 11th December 1841 to accept a treaty in which they promised to leave the country without delay. Their ally on the throne did not survive their departure; he was killed by his fellow countrymen. Not until 1878 did the British once again attempt to compel Amir Shah to recognize their protectorate. The enlightened emir, who had published a newspaper, *Shamsul Nihar*, in the Persian language, and had at the same time begun modern postal communications, was defeated. His successor had to acknowledge, in the Peace of Gandomak of 26th May of the same year, that he would listen to the counsel of the British in external affairs. However, the minor war against the British did not cease. Britain therefore had the sense to learn from the behaviour of the freedom-loving people. Whilst from 1872 onwards, British and Russians defined the northern frontier of Afghanistan, and in 1883 the Oxus–Amu-Darya was accepted as the Russian-Afghan frontier, the British-Afghan negotiations lasted until 1903, when the so-called Durand line defined the subsequent frontier between British India and Afghanistan. At that time the Pashtu-Afghan-speaking parts of present-day Pakistan fell into the hands of the British. Thereby the actual Afghan racial territory was divided, and it was then that the modern question, Pathanistan or Pakhtunistan, actually first arose, that question which for a long time troubled the relations between Karachi and Kabul and which made many of the Pathans advocates of the contested territory, the old North-West Province, as, for example, Abdul Ghaffar Khan, known as the 'frontier Gandhi'.

The exact settlement of the international status of Afghanistan, however, took place in the Russo-British convention of 18th August 1907 (31st August according to the Western calendar), when London and St Petersburg agreed on their spheres of interest in Persia, Afghanistan and Tibet. The article dealing with Afghanistan read:

The Government of His Britannic Majesty declares its intention not to change the political status of Afghanistan.

The Government of His Britannic Majesty feels under an obligation to exercise its influence in Afghanistan only by peaceful means, and it will never allow Afghanistan to take any measures threatening Russia.

The Russian Government for its part declares that it regards Afghanistan as lying outside the Russian sphere of influence and undertakes to conduct all its relations with Afghanistan through the representative of His Britannic Majesty; furthermore, it will send no representative to Afghanistan.

During the First World War an intermezzo was played by Germany, India and Afghanistan which is generally forgotten by historians of this period. A mission dispatched in 1915 from Turkey straight across Persia to Afghanistan has claimed rather the interest of young people who are intoxicated by absorbing tales of bold expeditions into unknown regions. And how colourful is the 'second Anabasis', the story of this expedition to Afghanistan by Oskar von Niedermayer, who appeared as *Hajji Mirza*, the pilgrim to Mecca, in the midst of the expedition of Indians, Turks and Germans. Mindful of the position of Afghanistan and of its historical role as the land of Mohammed of Ghazni and his spiritual followers, the Germans wanted to strike, through this country, at British power in India. It is true that the king would not have anything to do with the prospect of causing unrest in India of his own accord. Niedermayer writes: 'In the course of our subsequent negotiations I had to think again and again of a splendid image which he once used in conversation. He compared us to merchants with all kinds of wares, from among which he wanted to select those which seemed to him good and useful.' The testimony of an Indian, the aforementioned Rajah Mahendra Pratap, is also available on the subject of the same expedition, whose military conduct was in the hands of Ritter von Niedermayer whilst Dr von Hentig had charge of diplomacy. The Rajah writes in detail about this expedition in his autobiography. Nevertheless there proceeded from this circle a joint Indian-Afghan-German political entity: the proclamation which followed on 1st December 1915, of the first provisional government of India, in which the Rajah Mahendra Pratap appeared as president, Maulana Barkatullah as prime minister and Maulana Ubaidullah as minister of the interior. Both authors also describe in their books the internal political situation in Afghanistan. Here Niedermayer's remark upon the Afghan opinion of women is perhaps of interest:

In their attitude to women only a few Afghans were exceptional, amongst them the two princes Inajetullah and Amanullah, who were

Head of man from Sikkim, by Hans Gehrt, who spent four
years painting in the Himalayas

The Golden Temple of the Sikhs at Amritsar

married to the daughters of the enlightened Mahmud Tersi from Syria, the editor of the only Afghan newspaper.

Prince Amanullah, cited as being so modern, ascended the throne on 23rd February 1919. On 3rd March he informed the Viceroy of India of this fact, and demanded in the name of his 'free and independent government' the revision of the existing agreement. The answer from India was very cool. Thereupon King Amanullah marched his troops towards the Khyber Pass, and exactly two months after the communication to the viceroy, on 3rd May, fighting began between the British and the Afghans. However, a way of solving the problem of Afghanistan was quickly found. By the Peace of Rawalpindi on 8th August 1919, Great Britain recognized the complete independence of the Afghans. The successes which Amanullah was able to show in foreign and military affairs were not able, however, to make his internal political aims acceptable. His programme of reform brought the enmity of orthodox circles upon the far-sighted king. But Afghanistan's journey to the modern epoch had begun, and the successors of the reforming king have continued more wisely and swiftly what Amanullah with all his dynamic power wanted to complete immediately.

The history of Afghanistan travels a long road full of battles and wars. It is a road of expansions and military waves which overflowed again and again on to the plains. Today the country has a different programme: it is dedicated to an armed neutrality, and its great example is Switzerland. Just like William Tell's compatriots, the Afghans preserve virtues which make it difficult for a conqueror to overcome them. Afghanistan is aware of its strength, but still more aware of its weakness. The country is easily accessible to the north of the Hindu Kush, and therefore good relations with the Soviet Union are necessary for Kabul. The Protocol of Tashkent, dated 29th September 1948, ended the long-standing activities of the frontier commission. It is in its way a completion of the treaties of neutrality and non-aggression of 24th June 1931 and 13th June 1946. The question of Pakhtunistan is still unsolved between Pakistan and Afghanistan, but the visit of the King of Afghanistan to Karachi in February 1958 has helped to create a better atmosphere.

However, this royal visit was only an interlude. Ever since the

H

short stay of Nikita Khrushchev at Kabul early in March 1960, where he demanded in the joint name of Afghanistan and the Soviet Union a solution of the Pakhtunistan problem, this problem has been troubling the relationship of the two Mohammedan neighbours. The Prime Minister, Sardar Mohammed Daud Khan, attempted to explain the meaning of this problem for Afghanistan in the course of his visit to the Federal Republic of Germany and to Great Britain in June 1961, appealing in London to the good offices of the British Government 'as a mutual friend' in clarifying the situation on the Durand Line.

In the Afro-Asian community of nations Afghanistan plays a part which perhaps consciously renounces any great political demonstrations. Here too the country really is like Switzerland. Anyone who sees the Prussian cut of its soldiers' uniforms, and can admire the knowledge of English, French, German, and even Russian, of its students, must feel that armed neutrality also includes close acquaintance with foreign countries. When one walks along the clean streets of the capital and converses with the people, who talk to foreigners without the slightest feeling of inferiority, then one knows that the people of this country are taking their fate into their own hands, and wish to do so. And suddenly one senses how right are the words of that poet who speaks of Asia as 'a form made of clay and water', and calls Afghanistan 'the heart of this being':

> Asiya yek paikar-ábogil ast;
> Millat-i-Afghan drin paiker dilast.

10

The Saga of Turkestan

FACTORIES GROWING UP IN
THE STEPPES

THERE is no sight more memorable than that of the eternal
mountains of Hindu Kush in their austere beauty. Like some
imaginary landscape plunging into an unearthly white, lie the
snow-capped mountains, and the aeroplane glides over them.
Other passengers are suddenly far, far away. The link with time
and space is rent asunder, as dross falls, clinging to the earth.
Only the mountain peaks gaze—gaze, stretching upwards as
though formed by the dynamic will power of Titans storming
the heavens. What a splendid thing it must be to attack these
heights with one's own strength and to conquer them!

There is soon an end of dreaming. Plains covered with sand and
scrub suddenly appear in the north. The Amu-Darya flows lazily
below us. The ancients called it the Oxus and wove a wreath of
gay oriental legends around it.

However, this land of deserts and steppes mingled with oases
like bright spots of green and brown paint is too tough and manly
to be influenced by the recollection of legends. Rather it is a saga
written by conquerors: conquerors on horseback who once made
the world tremble and who today attack the terrible deserts and
steppes, so as to make them useful to mankind.

Turkestan is today divided politically. The two great powers
of the Communist sphere have here entered into the inheritance
once built up by emperors in Central Asia.

The great European expansion of the last two hundred years,

which sent a thronging stream of men to America or sought for the spirit of industrial enterprise new shores or outlet markets for rapidly expanding economies, had pressing internal causes. Russia, with her urge for expansion which had been active since Peter the Great, and who had always turned in the first place towards the West, seeking Europe and the open sea, found in her drive to the east only a military justification. Even if it is interpreted as a reaction against the Mongolian and Tartar period, this justification remains.

The first route of the Russians had been directly to the east. As early as 1649 the first Russian expeditions were by the Sea of Okhotsk. Not until two hundred years later did they strike out in a south-easterly direction from the Orenburg Gate. It began in 1839 with the subjection of the Kirgiz. In 1845 and 1846 the chain of fortresses—Kopal, Orenburgsk (Turgai), Uralsk (Irgis) and Alexandrovsk—was constructed. In 1847 the Emperor Nicholas ordered the building of Fort Raimsk (Aralsk) on the lower Syr-Darya. This was done against the advice of General Obrutchev, the expert on Turkestan. It brought Russia into the middle of Turanian territory. Contact with the Turkish Khanate was simply unavoidable.

This Russian probing alarmed the British. On 8th December 1864 the Russian chancellor, Prince Gortchakov, sent a soothing note to London, in which the tsarist measures in Central Asia were explained in relation to the particular situation. It was necessary to proceed differently with warlike races of conquerors than with peace-loving tribes:

Therefrom arises the necessity for new, expensive, repeated expeditions against an enemy who is rendered unassailable by his organization. Every step forwards leads to more steps, every difficulty overcome leads to new difficulties. But there is no retreating, for the Asians would regard that as weakness.

Russia kept to this policy of 'no retreating'. In 1865 Russian troops marched into Tashkent. However, the march continued farther to the south, and in 1867 the general government of Turkestan was formed from the Turanian regions so far occupied. A year later the Tsar's armies were in conflict with the mercenaries of the Emir of Bokhara. In the process Samarkand, the ancient city of the Timurids, fell into their hands.

The British were afraid that the Russian attack would not stop even at the frontier of Afghanistan, and proposed that this state should be considered a buffer state. This was established in the notes from Lord Granville (17th October 1872) and Prince Gortchakov (31st January 1873). However, the struggle for the Turkish Khanates was entering its final stages. First the Russians marched from the Bay of Krasnovodsk, which had fallen into their hands in 1869 and where one of their strongest fortresses was situated, against the Khan of Khiva in order to bring him to heel. By the Peace of Gandemian on 24th August 1873 the Khan renounced all possessions on the right bank of the Amu-Darya, and accepted Russia as a protecting power. The Emir of Bokhara submitted in precisely the same way, and his territory was likewise greatly reduced; and like Khiva he adapted himself to the 'new order in Turkestan' in a frontier treaty dated 10th October 1873. The new conquests to the east of the Amu-Darya and the lake of Aral were placed under the Russian 'general government of Turkestan'. However, the government of St Petersburg, by an order dated 21st March 1874, placed the so-called Trans-Caspian region under the control of the Caspian possessions lying opposite.

Finally, Russia demonstrated further to the Turkish princes how dangerous it was to oppose the tsars. In 1875 disturbances broke out in Kokand and the holy war against Russia was proclaimed. Thereupon the Governor-General's troops moved into the Khanate of Kokand, unceremoniously deposed the prince and attached his dominion to the province of Ferghana within Russian Turkestan. The subjection of the Kirgis of Kara in 1876, the Turkmens of Tekke in 1881 and the Mervs in 1884 satisfied the Russian expansionist urge for the time being. The Anglo-Russian endeavours to define the Pamir frontier between 1891 and 1895 and persisting until 1907 brought for the first time a breathing space in the struggle for Asia, which had consisted first of all in the 'race' for the foothills, the *glacis*.

This tsarist map of Central Asia was valid until the October Revolution, but in 1917 the Moslems of the Turanian provinces proclaimed an 'autonomous Turkestan' in the city of Kokand. Lenin—so it was said—wanted freedom for all peoples, wanted them to be internally and externally independent. One of those who believed this news was Enver Pasha, the former chief of the general staff of the Osman Turkish Army. This officer, who was

also the son-in-law of the Turkish Sultan-Caliph, was being prose-
cuted in Turkey at the time of the collapse, while the Turkish
tribes of Central Asia were celebrating their newly won freedom.
In 1919, however, Enver succeeded in escaping to Russia. He was
received in audience by Lenin on 12th February 1920, which
quickly became known amongst the Moslems of Russia. Enver
Pasha travelled to Baku to the congress of oriental races as the
personal representative of the 'father of the Russian revolution'
and was the star of the congress. Enver enjoyed his popularity and
soon the saga of this high-ranking Osman officer spread through
all the dwellings of Turkestan.

In November 1921 he went to Bokhara, the capital of the old
Emirate. Here he was received with enthusiasm. In the meantime Enver had learnt that the aim of the Soviet Russians was the
reoccupation of Turkestan, and that a free Turanian state would be
nothing but an illusion. Then he collected an Afghan bodyguard
and looked for volunteers to fight against the Russians. Only six
months earlier he had himself suppressed an anti-Soviet revolt
in the Turkmen province, and now he was working from Uzbek
territory for a free and independent Turkestan. He offered the
commander of the Red Army an armistice so as to negotiate on
the question of Turkestan. But the leader of the Bolshevik soldiers
refused, and so it came to bitter struggles. The Emir of Bokhara,
who had previously fled to Afghanistan, supported Enver; from
Bokhara he offered the caliphate, which was becoming weaker and
weaker on its home ground, a refuge in Turkestan. Among his
followers were the so-called Basmatchi—the fighters for freedom,
whose best-known leader was Ibrahim Beg. Enver, who had a
great deal of success and was soon master of Turkestan, then
committed an error which was speedily to thrust him from the
throne of his desires. He disregarded the wishes of the Emir of
Bokhara and deposed the somewhat obstinate leaders of the
Basmatchi, such as Ibrahim Beg and Tugai-Saryf. The result was
that they waged war on their own account: against Enver and
against the Soviets. Turkestan would be in a state of unrest as
long as Enver lived. The Russians recognized this and so they
formed their own Cheka group under Agabekov, who was ordered
to 'liquidate' the leader of the great anti-Soviet rebellion. But
when it was discovered that he was protected in his headquarters,
a small village called Kafirnigan, by a bodyguard which was very

devoted to him, two regiments of Red cavalry were sent. However, Enver escaped. Chance decreed—so the former prisoner-of-war Gustav Krist reports—that by the spring of Ak-su in the neighbourhood of the *Kisch-lak* (village) of Arundar, he and his adjutant, Süküs-Bey, bumped into the leader of the Cheka group which had been sent out against him. They were both killed. With that the Pan-Turkish dream of Enver Pasha was over. Pan-Turanianism, which had flared up so suddenly, did not survive Enver's death. In his book *Les Noyers de l'Altenburg*, which appeared in Switzerland in 1943, André Malraux tells of the adventures of the Alsatian Vincent Berger as agent of Enver Pasha amongst the Turkish tribes of Central Asia. As a matter of fact some of the Basmatchi fought on for a time, as did Madamin-Beg, Irkash-Bey, and above all Ibrahim-Beg, who did not give up the struggle until 1931, when he fled abroad.

Today Turkestan is still a great battlefield. Large parts of the country, which became Russian in the thirties of the last century, consisted of steppes and had first of all to be ploughed up. Cultivation was restricted almost entirely to the oases. This enormous Russian colonial empire—one must realize that from 1861 to 1876 in Turkestan alone, 1,048,178 sq. km. of land came under the rule of the Tsar—has become a school for Soviet youth to learn to do without and to make sacrifices. Today a planned stream of emigrants is directed through the Orenburg Gate towards Turkestan, and the girdle of the steppes which is Kazakhstan becomes narrower and narrower. On the other hand, however, more and more factories are springing up in the territories of the five Central Asian Soviet Republics, Kazakhstan, Uzbekistan, Turkmenistan, Kirgizistan and Tadzhikistan. The industrial area of Kuznetsk is already closely linked to the newly rising industrial development of Turkestan. Since the seizure of power by the Chinese Communists, which in Stalin's words represented 'a hammer-blow against imperialism', the vision of a great industrial area for Turkestan is made manifest. Chinese Turkestan, also called Sinkiang, and like Russian Turkestan inhabited by Turkish tribes, is destined by the decision of Peking to become an industrial area, corresponding to its Soviet Russian counterpart.

Of course one must not exaggerate the position in Turkestan. It is not that a hypermodern industrial area was suddenly made out of a country consisting previously of free nomads. Turkestan is still a country with agricultural characteristics and will long remain so. But the revolutionary aspect in this part of Central Asia is that the spirit of industrialization is being promoted, that the search for metals and minerals and oil is being made, that engineering works and cotton mills are rising up, that coal production has been increased, that the north-east of Turkestan in particular has today become a centre of the metal and machine industry; and finally that the Soviet industrial schools have a strong attraction for young people.

It must not be forgotten that 'Great' Turkestan taken as a whole has an area seven times that of the Germany of 1937. Industrialization can be carried out here without affecting the character of this large area. But just as formerly in the desert area, oases of agricultural tribes displayed a form of economy quite different from that of the remaining land which consisted mainly of steppes and to a large extent of desert, so there are today, in addition to and beside these agricultural oases, the industrial zones. In one of the republics, Uzbekistan, the production of industrial goods had in 1950 already surpassed the figures of 1940 by 89 per cent, and the production of these industries is still increasing.

On 14th February 1950 the Russians concluded a pact of friendship, alliance and assistance with the Chinese, whereby Soviet technicians also help to build up industry in Chinese Turkestan. On 12th October 1954 seven Soviet-Chinese agreements were signed, which were also partly concerned with Chinese Turkestan (Sinkiang). Of four mixed Soviet-Chinese societies, which were built upon a basis of equality, the Soviet shares were given to the People's Republic of China—1st January 1955 was fixed as the date of transfer. In the case of Sinkiang it was a question of the 'Society for the exploitation of non-ferrous and rare metals in the province of Sinkiang of the People's Republic of China' and the 'Society for obtaining and processing petroleum in the province of Sinkiang of the People's Republic of China'.

Another Chinese Soviet communiqué published at the same time as the other agreements announced a closer connection between Soviet and Chinese Turkestan through the construction of a railway:

In order to strengthen their mutual economic and cultural relations, the governments of the Union of Soviet Socialist Republics and the government of the People's Republic of China have agreed that both

sides will in the near future begin the construction of a railway from
Lanchow via Urumchi in Chinese territory to Alma-Ata in Soviet
territory. The Chinese Government will undertake the construction of
this railway in Chinese territory and the Soviet Government will undertake the construction in Soviet territory. In the construction of the
above-mentioned railway on Chinese territory the Soviet Government
will provide all general technical assistance. The construction of the
section of this railway from Lanchow to Yumen in Chinese territory
was already begun in 1953.

The Soviet Russians have tried again and again to make Sinkiang
in particular a part of the Soviet Union and to join the parts of
Turkestan. If today they can give up all the political ambitions
which they had here 'for the sake of socialist friendship', as they
so much like to emphasize, and instead seek mutual economic
and industrial co-operation with the Chinese, and if they still
today cherish as a 'Utopia' the vision of a 'Central Asian Mining
Union', then we in the West should draw the conclusion from it.
For the London *Economist*, the simple lesson was already to be
drawn from the Soviet-Chinese agreement of 16th October 1954:

If the Soviet Union and China manage to bury their differences in
the interest of a common policy, then Britain and America (together
with the other countries of the free world) have no alternative but to
follow suit.

It is surprising what an important role Sinkiang plays in the
mind of Peking. It should not, however, be forgotten that it was
formerly Chiang Kai-shek who turned his gaze towards north-
west China. In his book *China's Fate*, he declared that the future
of his country depended on the development of this area. What
Chiang Kai-shek once wanted is now a matter of compulsion for
Mao Tse-tung's planners. What the American settlers once
created with their individual pioneering spirit, Peking now wants
to create with all the characteristics of a planning bureaucracy,
by means of Five Year Plans, Water Utilization Schemes,
Settlers' Departments, and Workers' Negotiating Committees,
in order to fill, as regards population and economy, the area of
Chinese Central Asia, which has been for so long a vacuum in
world politics.

Long ago, in the days when the 'Son of Heaven' still reigned
upon the dragon throne of Peking, Turkestan was so very far

from the imperial residence. Court officials and ministers who had fallen from favour were punished by deportation, which in the hardest case was felt to be as severe as the death penalty. There were three different kinds of banishment decreed by the emperor: Mantau, Manlau or Mankwau. The first was a three- to six-year exile to a neighbouring province, the second took the victim for perhaps fifteen years to Mongolia or Manchuria, and the third meant lifelong banishment to 'Hsi yü', the western territories. That meant Hsin Chiang (here written Sinkiang) or the 'New Province', as the country beyond the Yümen pass was called.

Chinese Turkestan, the nineteenth province of old China, had for long enough had to feel the competition of imperialism. The less interested the owners themselves, the Chinese, were in this country, the harder the two rivals in Central Asia, Russian and British, endeavoured to establish themselves here. During the Second World War the Americans, too, suddenly displayed interest in Sinkiang when American experts estimated the future annual oil production of this region at approximately eighty million gallons. At the same time they established a consulate in Urumchi, the capital of Sinkiang (also called Tihwa). Today only the Russians are officially represented in Sinkiang. In 1953, when India and Pakistan wanted to open consulates general in Kashgar, this was disallowed by the Chinese with the indication that Sinkiang was 'closed territory'.

Russia's interest in Central Asia has always been accompanied by an urgency and pressure forwards. Britain's interest was more that of a power forced onto the defensive knowing only one anxiety: to safeguard her rule in India. Therefore when, in the middle of the nineteenth century, Russia also began to take an interest in Sinkiang, she made use of the autonomist tendencies amongst the Moslems of this country, and supported Yakub Bey in setting up an 'East Turkish Khanate' which lay as a buffer state between the British and Russian spheres of interest. When it collapsed there began an inexorable 'secret war' of *agents provocateurs* who were able to transfer the struggle of the imperialist powers into the petty tribal feuds. For ten years, from 1871 to 1881, Russian troops even occupied a part of Sinkiang, the Ili region. The race for Chinese Turkestan ended in 1881 in a three-power compromise in which the whole of Sinkiang was recognized as Chinese territory abroad. However, the Russians managed to be still represented in Urumchi.

After the Second World War the Russian pressure against China shifted towards the Mongolian *glacis*, when Outer Mongolia, free since 1912, had to identify itself ideologically with the Soviet Union. However, Sinkiang was not completely forgotten. In Urumchi, Kuldja and Chuguchak, Soviet bureaux for trade and external affairs were opened immediately after the end of the war, although at that time there were still no diplomatic relations between the Soviet Union and China. When relations had been resumed, Soviet influence in eastern Turkestan increased still more. But when, in 1929, as a result of tension over the conditions of ownership on the East Chinese railway, relations between Nanking and Moscow were broken off, the Russians let their consulates in eastern Turkestan remain and made them the real centres of power of the country. Once more Great Britain felt herself threatened, and in 1931 there followed the great Turkish rebellion of Hami, which had as its aim the setting up of a great Moslem empire here in the old historical 'turntable of events' in Central Asia. Now the Russians attacked in force. They had sensed in West Turkestan how very enthusiastic the Turkish tribes of Central Asia were about such a plan. The rebellion was crushed but the troops remained behind as a 'guard for the consulate'. The Soviet account was presented on 31st October 1931. On this date the Soviet Union concluded a secret pact of assistance according to which Soviet advisers were assigned to all military and civil posts in the province. At the same time the Russians promised to construct a military academy and a flying school in Urumchi. Teachers and instructors were Soviet citizens only. At that time there began also the first wooing of East Turkestan students, who were invited to study in Moscow and Tashkent. Finally, the result was that in 1934 the autonomous Soviet Republic of Jurgustan (Jungaria) was proclaimed. The region became *de facto* Soviet territory on 25th March 1939, when the Soviet Altai army occupied Sinkiang and expelled all foreigners (British and Indian) from the country. Not until the autumn of 1941, when the Russo-German war seriously threatened Moscow and every soldier was needed, did Stalin quietly withdraw his troops. Chiang Kai-shek visited the province in 1942 and pronounced all the agreements made by the Sinkiang Government

with Soviet Russia to be null and void. Chiang's rediscovery of
Sinkiang was to benefit Mao Tse-tung only. Similarly the prudent
policy over minorities, which in 1912 gave official recognition to
the five races (Han—that is, Chinese, Manchus, Mongolians,
Tibetans and Moslems), has in fact borne Communist fruits.
When the question of Pakistan in India arose, it was Chiang who
granted the Moslems the status of a special religious group.
However, the *Hui-min*, the 'Moslem race', became the *Hui-
chiao-jen*, the 'faithful of Islam'.

Today Turkestan—both Soviet and Chinese—is still a country
of Turkish tribes. But just as the Khrushchev plan for increased
industrialization, and at the same time for winning arable land,
will bring new hordes of Slav settlers to the western half, so also
Mao declared his intention five years ago of bringing millions of
peasants and workers to Sinkiang. According to the most recent
statistics available on Sinkiang, published in 1946 by the provincial
government of the time, 222,401 of a total population of 4,011,336
were Chinese and 99,607 Mohammedans of Chinese origin who had
emigrated from (Old) China. However, the principal part of the
population consisted of the following six Turkish tribes: Uigurs
(2,988,528), Kazakhs (438,575), Uzbeks (10,224), Taranchi (79,296),
Kirgiz (69,923), Tartars (5,614). Amongst the other inhabitants
were Tadjiks (8,210), Mongolians (59,686), Sibo (10,626), Golon
(2,506), Manchu (762) and naturalized White Russians (19,392).
Since 1946, 800,000 Chinese are said to have emigrated to the
country. Today the time can already be foreseen when a country
completely part of China as regards population is made out of the
eastern Turkish land to which the emissaries of Abdul Hamid II
once brought the gospel of Pan-Islamism and to which later on
Enver Pasha sent his Pan-Turanian prophets.

If it comes to a closer interweaving of the economies of the
Greater Turkestan area, then there is no doubt that the greatest
weight is attached to Tashkent, the city which was once generously
planned by Kauffmann, the governor-general of German origin,
and which today is in area the largest city of the Soviet Union
after Moscow. This city, the capital of the Republic of Uzbekistan,
had 585,100 inhabitants in 1939, but in fact about 830,000 people
live there now. The gay pageant of all the races of the Soviet
Union is represented there. First of all, self-confident, the Uzbeks,
then come Russians, Ukrainians, neighbouring peoples from the

states of Kazakhstan, Kirgizistan, and Turkmenistan speaking a Turkish language, and the Indoeuropean-Iranian Tadjiks. A large number of Bashkirs and exiled Crimean Tartars likewise live here in Central Asia. And finally, it has become the home of the remaining Volga Germans, who, at the beginning of the Russo-German war, were struck off the political and ethnographical maps of the Soviet Union by an order of Stalin. The Caucasian and Kalmuk regions, which were similarly wiped out on account of collaboration with the Germans, and whose population was deported to Central Asia, have meanwhile been restored. Only the Volga Germans and Crimean Tartars are not yet allowed to return home. The Germans have made new careers for themselves as respected specialists on the collective farms. Besides these Germans, I found in Turkestan a small Sunni tribe called Afghan, who are very like the Indians in appearance. Their language is likewise Indo-Aryan. Doubtless this tiny race of traders has taken its name from Afghanistan, and I may perhaps give here a few words from the Afghan language: water, *pani*; day, *din*; night, *rat*; fire, *ak*; eye, *ank*. These Afghans have an interesting custom: after the death of the elder brother, the younger marries the widow. This Mosaic custom is found particularly amongst patriarchal tribes.

The Russians wanted to make something special out of their part of Turkestan: it was to become a 'shop window' for the whole continent, where one could see how different races live peacefully side by side, where nomads are introduced to modern industrial civilization, and lastly where Asia's problem of filling the food-bowl is solved. The Soviet Russians have always been conscious of the fact that Turkestan was to play the part of 'shop window'. After the political remoulding of Turkestan, *Pravda* was already writing on 7th May 1925:

> The nation of Tadzhikistan is the outpost of a new culture in the eyes of the millions of people who make up the bulk of the Orient and who are of the same origin as them but are still held by the chains of imperialism.

In this connection we must not forget one of the most important centres in which the ideological training of youth is carried on in the pattern which is to belong to the 'new culture'. It is the 'University of the Workers of the East'. Today it is called the

'Lenin Central Asian State University'. It was Lenin who wanted to create the intellectual magnet for Asians here in Tashkent, and to send out trained forces from here into the Asiatic countries. On 7th September 1920 he published the decree establishing the university. I was told that in 1960 the fortieth anniversary would be celebrated as a great event in Asia. Officially the university has eight 'classical' faculties—physics and mathematics, chemistry, biology, geology, geography, history, philology and law. But in addition there are the historical institutes attached to it, where special provinces are studied, such as 'Problems of Colonialism and the Colonial East'. At this educational centre there are Soviet students and non-Soviet Asiatic and African students. The larger population groups have their own departments and the curriculum is adapted to the home country of the students. In addition there are eight hundred students taking correspondence courses who have to report twice a year for examinations and then to collect their marks, from 1—very bad, to 5—very good. Attached to the university is among others the Institute of Oriental Languages. Thus the Soviet Union possesses in Tashkent the focal point of an ideological influence reaching out to the farthest regions of the oriental world and beyond, to the Afro-Asian world. The rector of the university is generally an Uzbek, but the pro-rector is almost always a Russian. In 1958 the rector was Abid Sadikovitch Sadivok, and his deputy was Leonid Nikolaievitch Babushkin.

In some of the higher schools the pupils must learn an oriental language in addition to the compulsory languages. This experiment began in Kazakhstan, where in Alma-Ata the pupils of Secondary School No. 12 begin Arabic in the second form and in a neighbouring school they begin Chinese. In South Kazakhstan the secondary school of Sari-Agach began Persian in the same form.

However, the universities are of course the most important places for transmitting information about the East from the Soviet point of view. In 1933 the pedagogic academy in Samarkand was reformed as the second university of Uzbekistan. Then there followed additional university foundations in the other Central Asian republics: Alma-Ata in Kazakhstan (15th January 1934), Stalinabad in Tadzhikistan (1st January 1948), Ashkhabad in Turkmenistan (14th July 1950) and Frunze in Kirgizistan (24th May 1954).

In general the Soviet cultural policy in the Orient has latterly 'adapted itself more and more to the problems of the day'. At the twentieth party congress Mikoyan strongly criticized Soviet oriental research. While the whole of the Orient was waking up at this time, one must confirm, according to his criticism, that the Soviet Oriental Institute was sleeping peacefully on. On 11th October 1956 there began in Tashkent a three-day congress of scholars of the Central Asian Soviet Republics. At this congress the party secretary Mukhitdin announced the following programme:

Research activity in the province of oriental studies must be greatly improved.

Instruction in the languages of oriental races is to be introduced in the secondary schools of the Central Asian Soviet Republics.

A syllabus covering the culture, history and language of the oriental races must be worked out.

Publications dealing with the different problems of oriental races and cultures must be increased.

The body of specialist orientalists must be enlarged.

Soviet achievements are to be publicized throughout the foreign parts of the Orient by means of press and radio to a far greater extent than previously.

On the basis of these recommendations the Tadzhik Babadjan Gafur was named in November 1956 as leader of the Oriental Institute in Moscow. The poet Mirsan Tursun Zade, well known in all parts of Turkestan, became meanwhile leader of the committee of solidarity of the countries of Asia and Africa, founded in Moscow on 20th May 1956. The strengthening of the Soviet Far Eastern policy also brought it about that the second Asiatic Writers' Congress met in Tashkent from 7th to 13th October 1958 (the first took place in New Delhi from 23rd to 28th December 1956).

These are all signs that the Russians have begun an increased programme of cultural propaganda. It is a part of their policy. A scientific discipline is placed completely at the service of political aims. However, it directs and is intended to direct the eyes of Asia and Africa towards Moscow. And today the roads to Moscow run through Tashkent, the second capital, the Asiatic centre of the Soviet Union. Characteristically it was from here that Khrushchev, on 14th January 1957, took up a strongly negative attitude to the American programme for the peoples of the Near East, which became known as the 'Eisenhower doctrine'. It is easier to speak to the peoples of Asia from Tashkent; Lenin in his day knew that. Do we in the West draw the proper conclusion from all this? It could only be to give all possible financial assistance to a free and independent policy of orientalist research. This alone can be the preliminary condition for a genuine endeavour to select from the cultural values material to unite the nations. Finally, however, such a study would also have to provide a scientific foundation for those who in the future will have to make political decisions on questions affecting the Afro-Asian nations.

The Maharanee of Bhutan

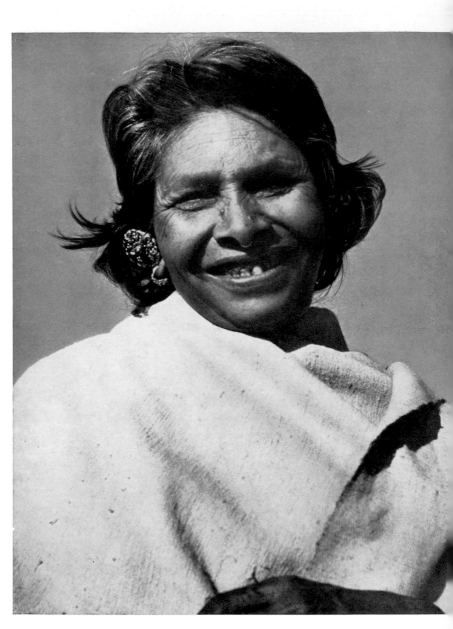

Woman from Nepal

11

Russian Interlude

WHITE AND RED TSARS HAVE ALWAYS GAZED BEYOND THE PAMIRS

PAMIRSKI! This word is like a pillar in the landscape of the intellectual visionary. '. . . of the Pamir. . . !' It was a programme, and the Russian philosopher who proposed to the emperor that he should add it to his hundreds of titles knew the power of the name and the title. Beside all the others: '. . . of Novgorod . . . of Pleskov . . .' and so on, this particular title would sound not like a historical reminiscence but like a programme, a gospel. The philosopher, Fyodorov, suddenly became a politician when this formula occurred to him. He was giving a universal claim to the Russian tsardom. The lord of the earth was to direct his peoples from the 'roof of the world', called *Bam-i-Duniah* over there in Turkestan.

The philosopher's proposal was only the expression of what many people were then thinking in Holy Russia. For thousands of years hordes of conquerors had descended from the Pamir Mountains and they must become the destiny of the land of the tsars.

Whether they were enraptured enthusiasts or quite clear-thinking politicians, the Russians have always been enormously fascinated by these mountains. They constituted a programme which was to be interpreted spiritually and carried out politically. That was in the time of the White tsars; with the Red ones politics and ideology went hand in hand.

The Empress Catherine II ('the Great'), of the princely house of
Anhalt-Zerbst, was already some years before her death studying
plans for an invasion of India. These proposals of 1791 envisaged
sending an army to India by way of Bokhara and Kabul. However,
according to Archibald R. Colquhoun, Peter the Great, who threw
open the window to the West, is supposed to have said, as early as
1722, when he stood on the shores of the Caspian Sea: 'In a twelve-
day march with pack-camels the route goes from here to Balkh and
Badakjan, and nobody can protest at this march against India.'

In the years when Napoleon Bonaparte was the First Consul of
France, the Tsar Paul I occupied himself with plans to push
forward towards India in league with France. He had already
given orders to General Orlov to march with his expeditionary
force to Orenburg. There exists a mass of documents from the
year 1801, when, however, the death of the Tsar destroyed all the
plans. However, many of them are rejected as false even by
historians who have specialized in this very period.

In 1808, a year after the Treaty of Tilsit, it was Napoleon who
called upon the ruler of all the Russians, Alexander I, to take part
in a joint campaign against India. Napoleon always dreamed of
following in the footsteps of Alexander the Great. He could not
forget the failure of his expedition against Egypt; and he wanted
to reach India. At the same time he had some idea of what must
be going on in the heart of Alexander of Russia. The Russians
had always regarded themselves as the heirs of the Byzantine
conception of empire, which saw in Alexander the Great the
mythical and historical ancestor of the Greek world mission.
Therefore the reply of the Russian Tsar was by no means negative:
'When we have arranged things in Turkey and in India, the British
will be compelled to make peace with us.' The conversations on
the future between the Russian and French emperors, which had
begun in a tiny East Prussian town, were to be abruptly cut off a
few years later by the Napoleonic invasion of Russia.

In the year 1808, however, Alexander I did not hesitate to come
to close grips with the problem of India. And so on 4th August
he sent Mekhti Rafailov to northern India. It was the first Russian
attempt to enter into relations with this country. Rafailov's
mission was to go to the court of Lahore, where the Maharajah
of the Sikh state of the Punjab resided. After his return from India,
Rafailov wrote a detailed report on his reception in Lahore. At

the same time he revealed himself as a close and critical observer of conditions in all the countries through which he travelled. In 1820, when he came once more to India and sought out the court of Lahore, the emperor had bestowed on him beforehand the title of privy councillor. However, on the way home the first Russian emissary to India died unexpectedly at Yarkand, in present-day Sinkiang. Thus ended this small diplomatic episode.

Russian historians do not in any way dispute certain ambitions in military circles to conquer India. They explain them only as the rattling of sabres by the governor-general in Turkestan or by some frontier commander or other. Officially Russia simply allowed them to behave like fools. No doubt there is some truth in this explanation, but equally there is as much that is false. Always it depends in what circumstances and in what atmosphere a word is let fall or a deed is performed.

Thus, when in 1839 General Perovski received the order to march against China, he saw this as the prelude to a march against India. In 1854 General Duhamel, and in 1878 General Skobelev, drew up plans concerned with future expeditions to India. The latter's project was published in 1883. It envisaged a march into the country beyond the Pamir in three columns, one of which was to advance in the direction of Chitral and Kashmir. Another Russian officer, V. T. Lebedev, emphasized the strategic importance of these very areas, and in 1898 in St Petersburg he propounded his plans in a book *V Indiu*.

While the military were committing sober plans to paper, Dostoyevsky was writing, in his *Journal of a Writer*, that the Russian was not only a European but also an Asiatic. But after the Russian victory over the Tekke-Turkmens he rejoiced:

May the news spread, may millions of people as far away as India become convinced that the White Tsar is unconquerable. . . . Such a conviction must be created. It is growing from year to year. We need it, for it will prepare them [the Indians] for the future.

The radical philosopher Constantin Leontiev, who—according to Sarkisyanz—valued the 'cultures of India, China and even Turkey more highly than those of the *bourgeois* North America and Western Europe', often expressed this valuation of the Asiatic world:

If we were to find by any chance, in Bengal or Tibet, Mongolians or Hindus headed by a strong and clever hierarchy, we ought to prefer this Mongolian or Indian hierarchy to a whole million Slavs with their liberal intelligentsia *à la* Gambetta. . . . We must prefer them. . . .

In view of this orientation towards Asia it was inevitable that Tolstoy would include Russia amongst the peoples of Asia, and that he once wrote that the role of the oriental races of China, Persia, Turkey, India, and Russia was to show the world the true way to freedom; or that Prince Esper Uchtomski, whom Sarkisyanz calls an intimate friend of the Emperor Nicholas II, once named 'the blue sea foaming round the continent' as Russia's frontier in Asia. The same Uchtomski, however, made himself the prophet of a fraternal unity between Russians and Asiatics. True authority must be brought to the peoples of the continent of Asia. The highest autocrat is the one anointed by God, and the Indians saw in him the personification of Vishnu and Shiva, the Chinese a reflection of heaven, the Japanese a descendant of the sun-goddess, the Mongolians and Tibetans the creative ray of Buddha:

Thus we finally recognize that the only fitting ruler of the East is the one on whose head the crowns of Perm, Jugor, the Volga-Bulgarians, Kazan, Astrakhan and Siberia gleam in fairy-tale splendour, united as one crown. . . .

In view of such an orientation southwards by a class biased towards the whole of Asia, it was inevitable that various attempts were made to establish contact. One such attempt was to set many a pen to paper for and against the person concerned. In 1889 the Maharajah of Kashmir, Pratap Singh, was accused of having entered into a treasonable correspondence with St Petersburg. It has not been proved what was accurate in this assertion or whether the protests of English authors such as William Digby were justified. However, the prince was immediately suspended, and was replaced by a council in his strategically important country. It was not until 1905 that full rights were restored to the Maharajah.

One of the first proclamations of the Council of People's Commissars shortly after the Bolshevik Revolution was the appeal of 3rd December 1917 to the 'Moslems of the East, Turks and Arabs, and to the Hindus!' In it was stated that the peoples addressed should throw off the yoke of imperialism and, helping each other, join the side of the Russian Revolution. In a similar manner, at the first congress of Eastern nations which opened the Third International in Baku at the beginning of September 1920, India in particular was addressed. It was Zinoviev who called upon the Indians to rise up in a holy war against the British.

At the second congress of the Third International in Moscow, the situation in China and in India was particularly examined. According to Korbel, Stalin is supposed to have seen in the Soviet-Afghan Treaty of February 1921, before the Executive Committee of the Third International in June of the same year, an instrument by which the Communist International could take up direct communication with the area farther south, with British India.

At the third congress of the Third International, Lenin spoke about the terror of the British in India. He also made his will in this sense. In it he regarded the victory of Communism over all other political systems as a foregone conclusion. On 4th March 1923, in his last article for *Pravda*, he made a kind of Asiatic balance-sheet: 'Our last analysis is that the end of the struggle will be decided by the fact that Russia, India, China and so on make up the overwhelming majority of the earth's population.'

It is a surprising political fact that Bolshevik Russia did not take note of the struggle for freedom waged by the Mahatma and his followers. This attitude towards India was to remain unchanged for a long time, and was expressed in the *Great Soviet Encyclopaedia*, which spoke of the reactionary doctrines of Gandhiism and wrote Gandhi off as a mere tool of Indian capitalists and landowners. When the Indians protested sharply, the section 'Gandhi' in Moscow's official encyclopaedia was finally altered. Moscow's attitude to India changed, however, after Stalin's death and after the end of the Korean War.

The Soviet Russians have cast a dense net of propaganda over Asia, especially over the non-Communist part of the continent. Countless publications appear in the different regional dialects and give reports and news in a way which has to appeal partly to unsophisticated readers. Then there are numbers of delegations; invitations to the Soviet Union are the order of the day. Schoolchildren, students and volunteers get free places in Soviet schools and in the factories of the Soviet Union.

The sort of romantic rapture of the nineteenth century has been replaced by a more realistic attitude on the part of those who today gaze over the Pamir Mountains. But somehow ideas survive amongst nations, just as what has once been really thought does not depart from the individual mind, but returns at some time or other from the subconscious to the conscious mind. So it will be in the end with those thoughts which may be blamed and criticized if they are recollected today. In their time they were once reality, as dreams and programmes can be reality. Thus the iridescent title *Pamirski* retains even for the Red tsars its realistic political significance, outwardly perhaps deprecated but secretly accepted.

12

Song of the Commonwealth

INDIA FORMS THE COMPROMISE LEAGUE OF STATES

Sat-chit-ananda is a classical formula of *Vedanta*, that Indian philosophy based on the assumption that a supreme world force is the origin of all doing and all being: *Sat*, being; *chit*, thought; *ananda*, happiness. In this way the words could be translated as single subjects, which as a whole, however, indicate the all-embracing, that which rules and guides the world. The word is like an image of the endeavour of Indian philosophers to formulate a conception embracing all things, and then to unite the factors which determine us into a principle. Just as Hinduism is a collection of an infinite number of philosophies, so the word *Satchitananda* compresses all words concerned with the divine into one word.

And this word shines like a light in the Hindu spiritual world: even Christians were inspired by it, e.g. those Christian missionaries who worked in southern India under Sanskrit names: Abbé Jules Monchanin (Swami Paramarubyananda) and Dom Henri Le Saux (Swami Abhishiktesvananda), who from their hermitage (Ashram) proclaimed *Satchitananda*, the Christian gospel with Sanskrit ideas, and, under this name, taught the secret of the most Holy Trinity.

The spiritual world of Hinduism is as all-embracing as a name can be which includes not only the highest being, God, but also all things upon earth. In the opinion of many of its interpreters Hinduism itself is reflected in this name. It is a spiritual structure,

built up over thousands of years, which is not held together by
the order of a dogma but has grown empirically. Its doctrines are
the sum of the experiences and communications of many wise
men. They have neither been given by a saint who is celebrated
as the founder of the religion, nor has God in human form proclaimed them. Hinduism is therefore a communion lacking what
other world religions have—a clear stamp of authority and thus of
tangible historical origins through their founder, and of dogma
valid at all times. Perhaps this is also the reason why a religious
syncretism, a fusion of the most contradictory philosophies, has
always been possible in Hinduism from the earliest times.
Hinduism does not embrace a clear system of thought, but has
become the vessel for so many different patterns. There are Hindus
who subscribe to the most diverse polytheism, and there are not a
few who have won through to a completely spiritualized monotheism. An atmosphere of synthesis leading to the middle way of
tolerance has grown out of the extremes brought together peacefully under the broad firmament of Hinduism.

This middle course of tolerance permeated all branches of
Indian life. It led through religious spheres and finally also through
political ones.

Therefore when the Indians were fighting for the freedom of
their country, the struggle did not assume the forms which were
often to be seen elsewhere when the oppressed rose up against their
former masters. A whole nation dedicated itself to the way of non-
violence, and set mind and spirit against guns and sabres. This
formulation may sound too precise, but it was this attitude which
provided the driving force in India's liberation.

Then, when India became free, and the division of this Indian
empire into the three states, the Union of India (called *Bharat* in
Hindi), Pakistan and Ceylon introduced the new era between the
Himalayas and Cape Comorin, the departure of Great Britain
was not accompanied by the outbursts of hatred usual in former
colonial territories. The colonial overlords of yesterday became
partners. This is doubtless the merit of the Indians, met half way
by British common sense.

And when today in New Delhi, the city planned for the British
by Sir Edward Lutyens, an Indian parliament meets and includes
a *Lok Sabha* (Lower House), and *Rajya Sabha* (Upper House),
then we are witnessing the influence here on the River Jumna of

the spirit of Westminster, that place on the Thames where for the first time Simon de Montfort called together burgesses and barons for the first Parliament, on 20th January 1265.

India—that is the Union of India—began the transition to independence first as a dominion, the last viceroy, who became the first governor-general, being a member of the British royal family. His successor was one of the faithful followers of the Mahatma, who bore merely the title of governor-general. This period as a dominion from 15th August 1947 to 26th January 1950 was at the same time a period of inner integration. The incorporation of the Indian princely states into the Indian Union was the work of Vallabhbhai Patel, who ranks as the 'Bismarck of India' in the history of his country. He created four different groups of states, which together formed the union of the federal state of India. They were first of all the 'A' states, made up of the former British provinces of the empire. Then came the 'B' states, the former great principalities, or amalgamations of former princely territories. The third group, the 'C' states, were smaller regions which had once had royal rulers and were placed on the same footing as the 'centrally administered areas' dating from the period of British rule, which were governed in a similar way. Finally the fourth group, 'D', consisted of territories completely subject to the central government (Nicobar and Andaman). The states which had grown out of former provinces were subject to a governor, but the president of a former principality or union of principalities of category 'B' was the so-called *Rajpramukh* (viceroy), and his deputy was called *Uparajpramukh*. The senior prince or former prince of the territory, according to circumstances, was provided with title and office. Thus an intermediate stage had been found between the age of the monarchy and the republican system. The heads of 'C' and 'D' territories were the chief commissioners and commissioners sent from Delhi. Kashmir, however, had a special position and still enjoys a special status. Its head is called *Sadr-i-riyasat* ('Head of State'). The president of the state still has this title today, and his country has its own constitution.

The remaining 'B' states disappeared, however, after the reorganization of the Union of India on 1st November 1956. At that time states were formed according to language. Some, e.g. Bombay, still have to be modified, but they slowly extinguished the memory of monarchic India. Since 26th January 1950 India has been a republic and obtained thereby a more unified internal political form.

The way to republican status was long. The proclamation was made exactly twenty years after the solemn vow of the Indian fighters for freedom that they would do everything for the independence of their country. At the same time they expressly bound themselves not to win their freedom by violence. Rajendra Prasad was elected first president of the republic.

The Indian constitution, consisting of twenty-two parts, determines the form and construction of the state in 395 Articles and nine Appendices. Constitutional authorities worked on it for years and closely studied Western constitutions. In particular, the traditions of Australia, Canada and Switzerland were sponsors of this unique attempt to remould in accordance with modern ideas a state previously organized according to class, caste and religious communities, which had partly assumed the character of national groups. The statutes of the Federal German Republic were also examined, to see whether they contained political propositions applicable to India. Amongst others, the principles in the Indian constitution dealing with the inviolability of the person are drawn from the German statute. Basic rights are divided into four groups in the Indian constitution: the right to equality before the law, the right to freedom and the law against exploitation, the right to education and freedom of religion, and finally the right to property.

When the Union of India decided to become a republic, the question whether to leave the Commonwealth or not was debated in New Delhi. For only one thing formally united all the Commonwealth nations, namely, the principle of the monarchy; that is to say the British crown of St Edward was the ruler's diadem which shone above all the partner states of this union.

However, the Indians found a means of combining both a republican outlook and loyalty to the Commonwealth. At the Commonwealth Conference in April 1949 Prime Minister Jawaharlal Nehru informed his colleagues from the other member states that India would shortly give herself a constitution and form a sovereign independent republic. He declared and confirmed in the name of his government that India wished 'to maintain her full membership of the Commonwealth of Nations and to recognize the king as a symbol of the free union of its independent states and thus as head of the Commonwealth'.

India had found the golden mean, and the ex-'colonials' had shown themselves stronger than those who put their faith in the former ruling class. The result was a much closer co-operation between India and the other Commonwealth countries. It is true that relations with two of them are troubled: with Pakistan because of the question of Kashmir, still unsolved after almost twelve years, and with the Union of South Africa because of their policy of *apartheid*, which affects the position of the Indians, especially in the country where Mohandas Karamchand Gandhi began his political activity.

The Colombo Plan, evolved at the 'last Imperial Conference' of British, New Zealand and Australian economists and diplomats in Canberra, established the partnership of the Commonwealth States long before the credit policy became a part of world diplomacy. The 'Nuclear Power Development Scheme', co-operation in the field of atomic development, is part of the plan, and to it India owes her first atomic reactor, a gift from Canada. To this scheme belongs also the great Indian steel works of Durgapur, built by Great Britain (the second, Rourkela, is a German project and the third, Bhilai, a Russian one). Harold Macmillan was the first British Prime Minister to visit India while in office, and on 11th January 1958 the *Times of India* published an eight-page special supplement: 'British Prime Minister's Visit to India.' A year earlier almost to the day—13th January 1957—the same paper had examined India's links with the Commonwealth. It was stressed that history knew no parallel example of the link between a former subject territory and the Motherland. The examples of the United States of America, the Irish Free State, the Philippines, Indonesia and Burma were quoted. The political present, with its balance of power in Washington and Moscow, had shown that India's decision to remain a member of the Commonwealth was the right one. Even the British Suez adventure, embarked upon without informing the other members of the Commonwealth, was no argument against it, for the reaction of the British people had shown a genuinely new attitude in Great Britain towards many Asian affairs. In any case the editor stressed that the 'economic personality of the Commonwealth' was quite different from the political one. Neither the Sterling Area nor strategic planning made up the Commonwealth, but it was a development according to logical points of view, in order to deliberate. The article bore the significant heading: 'History has Proved the Wisdom of Staying in the Commonwealth.'

A question of the Commonwealth connection is doubtless the language problem. There is a strong current of opinion among Indian intellectuals towards keeping English as the official language. The supporters of the policy of maintaining the English language come, amongst other places, from Bengal and the Dravidian south. In these circles it is pointed out, for example, that 'Indian English' is on the way to becoming a special branch of the Anglo-Saxon language group. This Indian element in the English language has its own individual expressions, such as 'I am coming from Bombay side . . .'; or in the pronounciation of *th*, as *tin* for *thin*, and in intonation. For example, 'What did he say?' ends for most Indians with a falling note, unlike standard English, but corresponding roughly to the Hindi 'Voh kya bolte?' The form of the sentence, too, according to which a statement in English is too often turned into a question by means of the so-called interrogative particle, has an Indian variation. Instead of the usual English, 'You saw him yesterday, didn't you?' there is in India, 'You saw him yesterday, isn't it?' giving to the English ear a faintly Welsh tinge to Indian speech. All these little Indianisms show that English has native rights in India. This is proved by an Anglo-Indian literature including such names as Rammohun Roy, Tagore, Sri Aurobindo, Nehru, Gandhi, Rajagopalachari, Radhakrishnan, and finally Kushwant Singh, Prawer Jhabvala, Kamala Markandaya and Krishnalal Shridharani. It is also proved by well-known newspapers which write brilliant English, such as the *Hindustan Times* (with S. Mulgaokar), the *Hindu* (with S. Parthasarathy), the *National Herald* (with Chalapathi Rau), and the *Times of India* (with Frank Moraes). The English-language press of India has won a high reputation for itself in the English-speaking world and has shown an individual development ever since 29th January 1780, when James Augustine Hickey with his *Bengal Gazette* published in Calcutta the first newspaper to be produced on Indian soil. As a matter of fact, in 1776 Wilhelm Bolts, a German in the employment of the East India Company, who had formerly belonged to the Imperial East India Society, had endeavoured to license a paper. The answer came promptly: he had to leave Bengal.

India's Commonwealth ties have worked favourably for the

large numbers of Indians resident in various parts of the Commonwealth. On 14th July 1948 an agreement was signed by the British
and Indian governments, which gives New Delhi the right to
maintain a commissioner in all colonies which have a large Indian
population. This is the case especially in the Fiji Islands, in
Mauritius, in Aden, in Guiana and in Kenya. The proportion
of Indians is also high in the West Indies and the Union of
South Africa.

Finally, there is a word from India's spiritual world which has
enriched the political vocabulary of the present. In the Indian
view this conception, like the compromise in the Commonwealth
which received its strongest impetus from New Delhi, should
contribute to the balance of power at the level of world politics.
This newly coined phrase for political literature and daily discussion is the most influential *terminus technicus* from the non-
Western sphere: *Panch-Shila*. This conception is a magic word,
suddenly presented to millions of people as a gospel to end the
confusion of this world rent by ideologies.

Today, wherever politicians from the Afro-Asian bloc appear,
they preach this simple lesson taken from the word *Panch-Shila*.
Just as the medieval Christians once preached *Treuga Dei* (the
'Truce of God'), in a world still enclosed in a catholicity of thought
and belief, just as the faithful of Islam made the 'land of peace'
(Dar-es-Salaam) a politico-religious aim, so the new, simple
political formula from India was to be a summons to the whole
world for all men to work together. Here the importance of living
together was stressed. The Communist doctrine had only proclaimed the happiness of one class. Other political doctrines—
such as the Monroe doctrine—had been directed merely to one
region or one continent.

The double word *Panch-Shila* comes from Sanskrit, and the
first part means 'five', the second 'rule'. We can translate *Panch-
Shila* into our political terminology as 'five principles'. These
are the five points which were the basis of the Tibetan Treaty
between the Union of India and the People's Republic of China.
These points, already outlined on page 38, were expressed in
plain and simple words which formulated the basic standards
which should apply between individuals and political and other
communities. However, the principles of *Panch-Shila* were soon
to become the most frequently played cards in the Asiatic political

game. The Asiatic viewpoint is often different from the Western one. So it happened that few Asiatics were aware that the largest Communist state had by that very means taken possession of a country with its own tradition and its own laws.

In the long run, however, Communist tactics have nothing to do with the honesty of India's plans for peace as expressed through the doctrine of *Panch-Shila*. The great variety of the religious and ethnological life of the Indian subcontinent has always compelled the Indian to seek a way of compromise and agreement. Indian philosophy naturally follows this path too. In the religious world it is so strong that synthesis and syncretism are an essential feature of Indian spiritual attitudes and religions.

India's new political gospel was preached for the first time before a world audience during the conference of twenty-nine Afro-Asian states in Bandung in Indonesia. The conference report of 19th April 1955 states:

In this battle of principles the *Panch-Shila* has been confused with the Indonesian *Panch-Shila*, which stands for Belief in God, Nationalism, Humanity, Social Justice and Democracy.

Thus two political doctrines each calling themselves '*Panch-Shila*' met in Bandung. The contradiction between them was again glossed over amongst some general proclamations and declarations in the final communiqué, of 24th April, without any information having been given as to where the difference lay. (The Communist delegates are said to have objected to the Indonesian formula 'Belief in God'.) The content of the Indonesian principles has already been mentioned briefly. *Panch-Shila* (written '*Pantja-sila*' in Malay) can here be interpreted as follows:

1. *Ke-Tuhan-an*, or Belief in God ('*Tuhan*' is an old Malay word for the Godhead).
2. *Ke-bengsa-an*, or Nationalism (the Sanskrit word '*Vamsa*' ('family') became in Malay *bengsa*, with the meaning 'people' or 'nation').
3. *Kemanusia-an*, or Feeling for Humanity (the Sanskrit word *manushya* ('man') was used in order to be able to translate 'humanity').
4. *Ke-adil-an*, or Justice, particularly Social Justice (in Arabic *adl* means 'justice').
5. *Ke-merdekan-an*, or Freedom, in particular Democracy (in Sanskrit *Maha-radhika* means 'Great Happiness', indicating the material basis of freedom).

On 1st June 1945 Dr Sukarno, later first President of Indonesia, outlined the spiritual image of the world in a speech significant for the political history of the present. He stressed that it was absolutely necessary to find an ideology for the future Indonesian state (the German word *Weltanschauung* appears again and again in his speech). It must be as inspiring as the Japanese attitude to the origin of the Tenno, long believed to be divine, as the faith of the supporters of Adolf Hitler, or of the people of the Soviet Union, or of the Chinese who followed the *San Min Chu I*, the Three Principles of the Father of the Chinese Republic, Sun Yat Sen. Europeans may be surprised that a few weeks after the German collapse Adolf Hitler's *Weltanschauung* should be used as a model anywhere in the world. However, here, as in the other cases mentioned, it was not the essence of the philosophies which was meant, but only the way of presenting a spiritual and political programme to the people that had fascinated the Asiatics.

In this speech Sukarno touched upon another essential point: the feeling which people have for the mythological. Five, he said, is a mystic number: there are five fingers on each hand, and in the physical world there are five elements. The religion of the prophet, Islam, recognizes five pillars. They are purifications, prayer, fasting, alms and pilgrimages to Mecca. In the Sanskrit epic *Mahabharata* five heroes were praised and they were known in every Indonesian village as *Pandava Lima* (five Pandavas).

In fact a modern and enlightened Asiatic was here drawing attention to something which is generally neglected by Westerners: namely the relationship between politics and myth. By 'myth' I mean the representation of ideas which identify feeling and spirit directly with cosmic, religious or primeval things.

Sukarno could have gone further. He could have said that the five-pointed star is the symbol of many Islamic states (in conjunction, of course, with the crescent of the moon), that the women of the Arabian Orient wear as an amulet a small hand with five outspread fingers, the 'hand of Fatima', that the magic number five travelled from the East to Europe and into the works of neo-Platonic writers, that as a pentagram it is supposed to give protection against evil spirits. The mystics of numbers ascribe a secret power to five, which consists of two, the dualism of man and woman, light and dark, and three, the trinity of earth, man and sky. This number was sacred: it banished the evil spirits of the night. Particular reference could be made to the *Panch-Shila* of the Buddhists, which had to be accepted by all the faithful: (1) Destroy no life. (2) Do not take what is not given to you. (3) Lead a pure life. (4) Do not lie. (5) Take no intoxicating drink. For Buddhist monks there were the *Dasa-Shila*, the 'Ten Commandments'. Then there was the Five-Fire doctrine for the Hindus. Amongst the Jains may be mentioned only the five *astikayas* (personifications of substances), the five *vratas* (promises), the five kinds of *samiti* (care), the five kinds of *gati* (conditions of life), the five kinds of *jnana* (wisdom), the five kinds of *charitra* (guidance). The Sikhs have five distinctive marks, the five K's: *Kesh*, the long hair wound into a knot; *Kangha*, the hair comb; *Kara*, the steel arm ring; *Kachch*, a pair of short trousers; *Kirpan*, the double-edged dagger. Even the *Cao-Dai* in Vietnam named five sources of their faith. The political followers of Abdul Ghaffar Khan were obliged to follow five commandments. The list could be extended at will. It proves how devoted Orientals are to the mystic number five. It may be one aspect of the success of *Panch-Shila*. The other is a psychological one, the need to support a gospel coming from a non-European source.

But whatever may be hidden in the subconscious, the underlying meaning of these principles must be recognized. It has no importance that one of the partners is perhaps more conscious of the propaganda value than of the moral obligation. But he signed something which he promised to keep, and that is no doubt a good deal.

We should recognize the true value of the *Panch-Shila* doctrine. Recognizing it also means evaluating it. We ought to see in India's political gospel an attempt to set about the solving of world problems in a simple manner. *Panch-Shila*, these principles born wholly of the spirit of India, are children of that spiritual world which has always sent gospels and doctrines to south-east Asia and the Far East.

India was the first Commonwealth state to recognize the People's Republic of China. It was because of India that the other members soon followed suit. The compromise state inside the union of states had tried to use her influence outside also.

The task which India took upon herself, first to become master of her own innumerable internal problems, and then to exert her influence abroad so as to win international recognition and give proper weight to her own ideas in the world, seems to the Indians to be like the task which Bhagirath once undertook. Therefore, when Indians mention their many problems, the Marathi-speaking Indians talk of *Bhagirath prayatna,* and those whose mother tongue is Malayalam speak of *Bhagirath yatnam.* This expression appears in all Indian dialects with a new significance; in Western terms it could be translated as a 'labour of Hercules' or 'task of Sisyphus'. This task and these problems are spiritual and intellectual, as battle has always been on Indian soil, ever since the struggle for this land began long ago on the mythical battlefield of *Kurukshetra.* Then burning questions arose as to meaning and purpose and the spiritual aims of things, and Arjuna received from Krishna the deep wisdom contained in the *Bhagavadgita;* and similarly today the whole world has become a great *Kurukshetra. Kurukshetra* was once also called *Dharmak-shetra* (battlefield), where there is a fight for right and justice. In the first place the decision is a spiritual one, and we have to discover how we can save the spirit, humanity, in our world-*Kurukshetra,* how we can give it a new dwelling-place of confidence and hope.

K

13

Sino-Indian Antiphony

ASIA CONSIDERS CHINA'S AND INDIA'S PROGRAMMES

IN 1924 an Indian poet visited China. Such a journey might usually be considered a literary event, but in this case it was more: it was a cultural encounter which was to have political consequences. Rabindranath Tagore was the discoverer of China. On the journey to China, at sea, on the rivers, travelling by train through the huge country, he wrote poems and notes on his journey faithfully conveying the charm which China can exercise over strangers. Translations of Chinese poetry into Bengali have helped to renew relations across the Himalayas. This journey to the Middle Kingdom had another outcome: the foundation of the China Bhavan, the Indo-Chinese Institute at the Tagore University of Vishna-Bharati at Santiniketan in Bengal.

For centuries relations across the Himalayas had been lively, but they were loosened in the Islamic period and forgotten in Asia's European era, because the peoples of the continent were confronted with new historical events and had to make a spiritual adaptation.

The first Indians to come to China are ascribed to the first century A.D. From the tenth year of Han Yung Tsin to the fifth year of Tang Chen Yuan—A.D. 87–789—about twenty-four Indian scholars visited the Middle Kingdom. In addition there were about thirteen learned men from Kashmir, which the Chinese did not then consider an Indian territory. During the time of the

136

dynasties of the Western Tsin to the Tang—roughly A.D. 265–790—quite the opposite, a far greater number of Chinese came to India to study. There were about 187 of them, of whom 105 are even identifiable. The best known amongst them were Fa Tian, Chemong, Sung Yu'n, I-Ching, and above all Hsiung-Tsiang, who stayed for sixteen years in India (629–45) and translated seventy-five Buddhist works into his native language. His journeys are still regarded as classical routes and the young people of China still trace them today, much as European young people once followed Marco Polo's journeys or today study those of a Sven Hedin. When Hsiung-Tsiang returned home, the emperor rewarded him with the highest honours.

The cultural stream now flowing towards China was almost endless. A Japanese-Buddhist lexicon once established that between the Han and the Tang periods more than thirty-five thousand words were newly created by Chinese Buddhists as a result of their preoccupation with Indian works. This new creation was brought about in two ways. Sometimes Indian words were taken over and given a Chinese pronunciation. Thus the Sanskrit word *Nirvana* became the Chinese *Ni-pan*. On the other hand, the Sanskrit *sattva* ('all living beings') was translated *Chung-Sen*.

But the spirit of India also transformed the outer form of literature in China. The Chinese ideograms which make up the writing in the Middle Kingdom were in part too complicated. As soon as Buddhism and Sanskrit had won a prominent position in Chinese intellectual life, the Indians, who, through Buddhism, had become critical observers, devised a simplification of the written signs. They invented fourteen symbols representing a Chinese alphabet. The Chinese called the Indian writing *Se-yo-hu-shu* or 'strange writing of the Western Countries', or also *Pa-laman-shu* ('Brahmin way of writing'). When the Chinese republic was proclaimed in 1911, this alphabet was to replace the ideogram form of writing. However, the alphabet proved again to be not modern enough, and the reform which the Indian Buddhist missionaries in China once began is today continued by pioneers in the art of writing—to mention only James Yen—who seek to make a popular writing from the scholars' script. At present the People's Republic of China is faced with the great problem of reforming the calligraphy. The transition to Roman letters will gradually be made by way of a simplified way of writing. Here it is interesting to note that Peking is not willing to accept the Cyrillic script which after 1936 the Soviet Russians had forced upon their peoples who had used the Roman instead of the Arabic characters.

Before the Buddhist 'discovery' of their country Chinese literature had often lacked system, logic and consistency. There is no doubt that they learned a great deal from Indian logic (*Hetuvidya*) and now found room for analytical and critical method. When Hsiung-Tsiang became an enthusiastic student of this part of Indian culture, an enrichment of the intellectual life of the whole of eastern Asia ensued.

Indian architecture also came to China along with Buddhism. Temples, *stupas* and grottoes for worship became indigenous in the Middle Kingdom. For example, according to ancient tradition the *Pa-Me-Se* in Loyang, the 'Monastery of the White Horse', is supposed to have been modelled on the architecture of the Anathapindarama in the Indian state of Kosala. Late examples of such buildings designed by architects from countries south of the Himalayas are, in Peking alone, the White Tower of the Miao-ying monastery, designed in 1348 by the Nepalese Anika, and the Temple of the Five Pagodas built in 1403 by the Indian Buddhist monk Pancha-Darma after the model of Buddh-gaya. China's pagodas, lying by silent lakes, on gentle hillsides or in crevassed mountains, have blended Indian and Chinese style and feeling in a splendid way. The architectural masterpieces have produced the most beautiful harmony in the interplay of the two cultures.

When one speaks of Sino-Indian architecture, one must also include the rock grottoes and their sanctuaries, which are seen in India, especially in Ellora and Ajanta, as stone-carved monuments of Buddhist piety. Yung-Kuang, Lung-Men and Tung-Hwan have the same significance for China as these sanctuaries have in the land of Buddha. The paintings from the caves of Tung-Huan were forgotten for centuries until Sir Aurel Stein rediscovered them.

At the beginning of the eighth century, when Buddhist monks began to revise the Chinese national calendar, they also influenced the astronomy of the Middle Kingdom. The Indian monk Gaudamara called his calendar *Dwang-Tse-Li* ('Calendar of the

Shining House'). That was in 715; but three years later the ruling Tang emperor received from the hands of another Indian called Siddhartha the translation of the Indian calendar *Navagraha-Siddharta*. For the Chinese this was henceforward the calendar *Kiu-Che-Li*. In about 721 the Chinese Buddhist Yi-hing introduced new calculations into Chinese astronomy. He also gave the number of planets as nine, which was contrary to Chinese opinion of the time, for they knew only seven.

The literary style was correspondingly influenced. A type of short story, previously unknown in China, established itself in literary circles. The Chinese themselves were acquainted with a kind of lithography. India gave them wood-block printing. The first book to be printed was done by this method, in 868. The book was the *Vajracohedika-prajna-paramita-sutra*. It should be briefly mentioned, however, that before this book was sent out into the world, something had been produced a century earlier in China which unaccountably had no lasting influence on China's development: namely, a newspaper. However incredible it may sound to Western ears, in the year 732, when Charles Martel halted the Arabs at Tours and Poitiers on their advance towards Central Europe, the Chinese Imperial Court Bulletin first appeared. Later it was published under various titles, including *King Pao*. Its first title was *Kai Yuan Shih Pao* ('Official Journal of the Government of Kai Yuan') and it appeared in Changan, present-day Sian, until 741. The last successor of these ancient newspapers did not finally perish in its modern form until 1925—fourteen years after the establishment of the Chinese Republic. However, there was already a forerunner of the modern press under Caesar, who published his *acta diurna* on wax tablets.

The Indian Buddhist influence was not lacking in pedagogic matters. Thus India's Ashram became China's Shu-yuan and this had the effect that Neo-Confucianism was less steeped in the material and more in the spiritual, and moreover became more philosophical and less political. This blending of Indian and Chinese cultures can be seen in the remotest spheres and can finally be traced right down to modern times.

India's many cultural gifts to China have given the people of the land of the Hwang-ho and the Yangtse-kiang the feeling that similar spiritual forms have met here at the crossroads of culture. Therefore it is understandable that China, seeming so ancient and almost fossilized to us, regards herself as a 'young nation' in comparison with India. Moreover the Japanese have the same feeling with regard to China. And so Liang Chi Chao, one of the former rectors of Peking University, an interpreter of ancient Chinese wisdom, expressed this feeling towards India in the preface to Tagore's *Talks in China*:

India and China are like twin brothers in both character and geography. Before most of the civilized races began to be active, we two brothers had already begun to study the problems of all mankind. We had already reached many conclusions for the good of humanity. But India was ahead of us, and we, the younger brother, followed him. However, Nature was not kind to us. She had laid between us a broad expanse of merciless desert and two great ranges of cruel, snow-covered mountains, which separated us for thousands of years. It was only about two thousand years ago that we gradually realized we had an elder brother on this earth.

As a matter of fact another country, the Soviet Union, now plays the part of brother in Communist China. The land of Lenin and Stalin, and of Khrushchev, is the home of the 'bigger brother', but the role of 'elder brother' is still reserved for India. The Chinese, leaning towards the Soviet Russians, are powerful in this age of Communist state alignment, but it is hardly credible that the Chinese will in future always allow the 'bigger brother' to have the last word in spiritual and ideological matters. China's national personality is too clearly stamped for that. At the moment, however, the marked inclination towards Soviet Russia must not be overlooked.

The 'younger brother', who like the 'elder' rebelled against European tutelage, worked out a solution different from India's after the rebellion. India fought a battle which was concerned at the same time with the soul of what was being fought for. China cast off all kinds of bonds by meeting might with force. From the struggle against strangers there grew a terrible civil war which destroyed the great family of Han.

And so the political outlook of the country to the north of the Himalayas is different from that of the world to the south of this mightiest of all mountain ranges. Today India and China go different ways, politically, spiritually and socially. The stress which is always laid on their common spiritual tradition cannot deceive us in this matter. Under Mao's Communist régime this tradition has suffered a severe shock for the first time in China's history. Until now all foreigners, even if they came as victors, have finally bowed before China's spiritual inheritance. This time no conquerors marched into the cities on the great rivers of the Chinese clay lands, but instead came a new doctrine: the ideology linked with the names of Marx and Engels, celebrated by Lenin and Stalin, which might be able to create something new and Chinese out of all the teaching of the German, Russian and Georgian prophets of world Communism. As regards administration and authority, the hand of time in the Kremlin in Moscow pointed backwards to the age of the Mongolian Tartars, and actually Peking has equally become once more the old Mongolian Khanate. Here the hard fist of an ideology in which the end justifies the means holds people and lands together. But down there in the Indian Moghul city of Delhi blows a wind of broad tolerance which has always been present since the first of Timur's race to show the other face of Mongolianism ruled there. One of their descendants had a golden proverb inscribed in his royal hall, saying that here was 'paradise on earth'.

Today others also on the other side of the Himalayas speak of the paradise on earth proclaimed by Shah Jehan in the Divan-i-Khas of the Red Fort of Delhi.

India, with a constitution recognizing tolerance and discussion, talk and struggle for spiritual understanding, and Communist China, where in the last analysis men are ruled by nothing but a cold ideology, are competing for a whole continent. They are the biggest states of the world. One of them is the largest in the world to know our idea of freedom. The other is the largest of those Eurasian mass states which are subject to the cult of the group which moulds them, and silently obey its orders.

The eyes of Asia are fixed upon these two countries. Who will bring home success, and will this success be properly valued? The people of a whole continent are considering the programmes of India and China.

Apart from regional variations, Asia's problems are almost everywhere the same. It is the problem of land reform and of an adaptation of the countries concerned to the modern industrial age. India wants to solve these questions slowly and organically, and so attempts are made in India, like that of Gandhi's follower, Vinoba Bhave, to improve the lot of the landless masses in the

500,000 villages by appealing to the heart of the landowning class. China solves her problems by force, and often does not hesitate to defend even the liquidation of rich landowners as a method answering the purpose or 'serving the people'.

In this connection it is worth reading what an Indian delegation studying the co-operative movement in Chinese agriculture had to report on its experiences after having made long journeys through China in 1956. In the *Report of the Indian Delegation to China on Agrarian Co-operatives*, published by the Planning Commission in New Delhi in May 1957, two different attitudes towards questions of land reform in the Chinese People's Republic can be traced.

A favourable account contained, among others, the following points.

The success of the Co-operative Movement in China was only possible thanks to the efforts of the people, in which the support of the whole machinery of government and of the party played a role. The incentive to individuals and groups was maintained by developing a system of evaluation of work which is known as 'norms' and which makes possible a fairly exact estimate of the quality and quantity of each piece of agricultural work carried out by an individual member. Each co-operative farm has its own 'norms' which are based upon the average achievement of an average worker. . . . Each co-operative farm has an elected leader, a few deputy leaders, a treasurer and an executive committee. It is always arranged that the leader or one of the deputies is a woman. We were very impressed by the leadership of the co-operative farms, which owe their success more to persuasion and conviction than to authority. . . . The success in China was very strongly influenced by the nature of the land reforms, which destroyed all traces of Kulak economy; land was given to all those who wished to work on it. . . . Nevertheless a co-operative movement would not have arisen if it had not been the considered policy of the Chinese Government and of the Communist Party to stimulate and strengthen this form of organization. First co-operative farms were formed by active members of the peasants' organizations and of the Communist Party, by whom the distribution of land in the villages was carried out. After an initial period of successful demonstration, a campaign was begun to arouse ideas of co-operation, and many peasants joined, not only for the sake of increased production and a higher standard of living, but also for rapid industrialization and the development of Socialism. . . . We feel that the great majority of the peasants joined the co-operative farms voluntarily. . . .

The following report was made on the Japanese co-operative movement:

The climate of Japan does not favour the development of agricultural co-operatives. Unlike the Chinese, the Japanese economy is based on the system of free enterprise and personal initiative. One of the compelling factors in the development of economic co-operatives is lacking, namely the desire to attain Socialism in the field of agricultural economy.

This very favourable judgment on Chinese collective farms caused part of the delegation to publish a minority report. In this 'Minute of Dissent' and arguments for this attitude, the report makes this and other points:

We maintain that the evaluation of the agrarian policy of the Chinese Communist Government, from the land reforms to the setting up of collective farms, can be fully understood only in the light of the dogma of Marxist-Leninist thought . . . the history of the establishment of the so-called co-operatives in China fully bears out what was said above. First the peasants' enthusiasm was fired by the slogan 'Land for the peasants!', so that the land owners could be destroyed; the peasants were then organized into the original co-operatives, during which time great stress was laid on the inviolability of the ownership of land and on a scale of compensation for their right of ownership. Finally they were robbed of all their rights of ownership, and in the name of Socialism were reduced to the status of wage-earners. We were therefore unable to share the enthusiasm of our colleagues who regard these tactics as progressive. From the very beginning this policy was used to lead the peasants into complete proletarianism. Chinese sources also admit this conclusion. . . . At as early a stage as 1951 it was made known in official Chinese statements that land reform was only the first step in a complete collectivization after the Soviet model. . . . It is not our intention in this short notice to describe the method used to extinguish the rule of the landowners ('landlordism'), which cannot by any stretch of the imagination be called civilized. A study of the local papers published in China in 1950, such as the *Yangtse Daily News* and the *Southern Daily News*, could satisfy the curiosity of anyone wishing for details. For the purposes of this report it is sufficient to repeat the words of Poyi Po, a member of the Central Committee, in an article in the *Cominform Journal* of 20th September 1952: 'In the past three years we have liquidated more than two million bandits. There are no more bandits in China and the social order is stable.' As bandits and landlords were often mentioned together, it may certainly be concluded that a large number of the two million bandits liquidated during the years of the land reform were landlords. . . . Our colleagues do not see the obvious contradiction between the recognition of the principle of free will and the simultaneous announcement of records in the number of co-operatives to be established from year to year. But how a 'voluntary' movement can develop according to planned targets fixed by the state is something which we cannot understand. . . . We are surprised and a little amused that our colleagues see more 'free will' about the establishment of these co-operatives than the Chinese do themselves. . . .

The *Southern Daily News* in Canton wrote: 'The peasants fear that their obligations will increase if production is raised. They fear collectivization of their land and their property. They live in fear of being considered rich and are therefore proud of being poor. The moderately well-to-do peasants have no interest in increasing their activity; rich peasants and landlords show no desire whatsoever to produce because they fear the attacks made against them.' (Nanfang Jih Pao, Canton, 29th June 1953.)

These extracts show sufficiently clearly that there was opposition on the part of the peasants to the formation of the co-operatives. . . . In our view the organization and the method of working the so-called peasant co-operatives are neither voluntary nor democratic. . . .

A few remarks on Japan continued in the 'Minute of Dissent' are given for the benefit of the reader:

Our colleagues have had only little attention to spare for the experiences of Japan, which in our opinion are of greater significance for us in India than the experiment in China. The average size of a holding in Japan is even smaller than in China, and doubtless much smaller than in many parts of India. And yet the Japanese have been capable of increasing the yield per acre within the last two decades in a remarkable way. Today Japan has the highest average yield per acre of rice in the whole of Asia. We found that the life and activity of the farmer in Japan are completely determined by the co-operatives—with the exception of the sphere of production. The co-operatives help the Japanese peasants with credit, buying and selling, and with legal procedure. . . . The structure of the credit system is closely linked with the system of buying and selling. At village level the co-operative unit is concerned with credit, buying and selling. But at the next level, the region, the credit system is separate from buying and selling. At regional level there are, in addition to the credit unions, unions for buying and selling. At state level the functions of buying and selling are again separated, and there are two unions, one the National Union of the Agricultural Co-operative Sales Society, called *Zenhunran*, and the other the National Purchasing Union, called *Zenkoran*. This is the type of co-operative which caters for the needs of the peasant in Japan.

Japanese experience shows clearly that a combination of peasant family
work and co-operative services with generous help from the welfare
state is the correct policy to introduce in order to raise the production
per acre in over-populated countries. No interest is shown in Japan for
communal work in production, and attempts to set up such co-operatives failed. In fact, when the peasants meet to discuss land reclamation,
they prefer to clear the fields as individual peasants, once they have
recognized the need. We believe that the things which raised produc-
tivity in Japan can without doubt be of great importance to us in India.
We do not share the opinion of our colleagues that co-operative services
cannot provide a solution of the basic problems of small farmers. . . .
We recommend that the multi-purpose society at village level should
be concerned with provision of credit, supply and communal market-
ing of agricultural products. These basic societies should be the pillars
on which the whole structure of co-operatives should be built, and if
he needs anything, the peasant should turn to the society. . . . Nevertheless we do not condemn communal work even in production, if it
came about in complete freedom, with the agreement and will of the
people. There are districts in India where communal co-operative
work on the part of the peasants should be attempted. Here we have
in mind particularly the undeveloped regions, for two reasons: (1) The
people there are accustomed to a communal life and would not find it
in any way revolutionary if they were put to work communally on the
land; and (2) where knowledge of agriculture and agricultural practice
is so small, agricultural co-operatives would be the simplest way of
giving them agricultural education. We would not condemn outright
communal land work for other districts also, in so far as the people
desire it. We are, however, of the opinion that the development of
co-operative farms should not be part of a government programme. . . .

If we have dealt with this subject in some detail, then there is
justification for it. Asia is still a continent of peasant workers and
small landowners. Apart from a few local variations, this is true
especially for all monsoon countries. Even the industrial zones of
Asia have, in spite of industrialization and modern techniques,
exactly the same land problems as other states. But that is just
why a searching inquiry into the questions facing Asia's peasants
is a necessity—even for us in the West. It is certainly not a matter
of no importance which way they set about solving the problems
of land and surplus population in Asia. The prophet of the voluntary surrender of land, Vinoba Bhave, calls upon his rich countrymen to give voluntarily and to solve the problems with their hearts.
According to him, the gift of land is not only the material gift, it

is more a service to mankind and at the same time the fulfilling of a divine commandment. Bhave acknowledges happily: 'The grace of God has caused unknown streams of pity and love to rise up in the hearts of the people of this ancient land, and with this help alone a New World is created.' Three points convince him that he has shown the way to this new world, and especially that it is the right way: 'My will is in harmony with the cultural tradition of India. It contains in itself the seeds of an economic and social revolution. And finally, it can help to ensure peace on earth.'

Enough has been said about the harmony between India and China which has lasted through the centuries. But even in the centuries when it was still possible to live together in a purely spiritual relationship, this harmony meant that China was searching for her own way. It is the way which separates religion and philosophy, and which is not India's, just as India, too, gave only an image of the Buddha and then took leave of it. The famous Chinese statesman and philosopher, Carsun Chang, spoke of this difference in his book *China and Gandhian India*:

In spite of these relationships and similarities India and China belong to two worlds. India's greatest desire is religion, whilst China's teaching is ethical and not religious. India has its caste system, China has tried to suppress class distinctions since the time of Confucius. If I may be allowed to modify a little Radhakrishna's division into Western thought and Eastern religion, I should like to add a third category, Chinese ethics or, in Kant's language, practical reason. Practical reason is closely linked on the one hand with pure reason, which gives us the all-embracing forms of knowledge, and on the other hand with the three ideas of the soul, of the world in its entirety, and God, which are the foundations of religion. In this sense one can say that China belongs neither to the province of Western thought nor to the category of Eastern religion, but that it lies between the two. Because of this central position China has to introduce Buddhism or other religions from outside and, in turn, modern science from Europe. The Chinese were trained by Confucius to have broad, open minds and not to be too exclusive.

China's desire was to follow the thoughtful, empirical, philosophical middle way. Dynamic outburst or religious ecstasy was not the aim of these people tamed by philosophy. It is symbolical that the 'Prometheus of the Chinese' was Sui Jen. But unlike the Western hero he did not fetch down fire from heaven. Sui Jen saw how a bird hammered with its beak on hard wood until the sparks flew. Thus he got fire as a simple gift in return for cool observation.

The Chinese Lin Yutang also bore witness to the difference between Chinese and Indians in his book *The Wisdom of India*:

It is characteristic of Indian thought that in India religion and philosophy cannot be separated. In India no link is necessary between philosophy and religion, and the problem of tracing this fatal missing link in the modern world does not exist. Hindu philosophy and knowledge of God are inseparable, as Chinese philosophy and questions of human behaviour are inseparable.

To this difference, which could once give a home to Buddhism in China but bar the entry of the really religious India, the true India, there is now added in our own day the caesura which cuts off all aspects of life in the old Middle Kingdom from their former spheres of activity, and would like to give them a completely new content. From Yunnan in the Chinese foothills of the Himalayas, the ancient home of the Thai peoples, from whence they conquered Laotian and Siamese territories, the peasant Communism of the poet-rebel Mao Tse-tung has overcome the whole of China after a long, tenacious struggle. And the questions which yesterday dealt with philosophical enlightenment and religious endeavour are asked in a similar way today. In the meantime, however, the philosophers of China have become ideologists, and the people in India, the land of religious searchers, know meanwhile that true religion can flourish only under the palm trees of freedom. China had often been ruled by despotic ideologies. A state under the Ch'in, who in the third century B.C. adopted the ruler's title of *Shi-huang-ti* ('First exalted emperor') was already acquainted with modern political co-ordination, burning of books and palaces with subterranean entries. Lin Tsin-Sen has described it all. And today China has a ruling class who, like the Ch'in long ago, have built up a state planned down to the smallest detail.

A well-known Indian economic journal, *The Eastern Economist*, drew an economic, cultural and political conclusion in an India-China number dated 3rd January 1958:

Do we want a system with such strong centralization as China has built up? Do we want the elimination of the private sector in faith, lest it should undermine the philosophy of the welfare state? Do we want free international relations or the closing of our frontiers to most countries of the earth, so as to play an inactive, and in the last analysis subordinate, part in the Communist union of nations? If such a choice were to be made, then it would deal a severe blow to the great moral prestige which India has won for herself in the world as the heir to the great gospels of Asoka and Mahatma Gandhi. In so far as these gospels are based on a moral law which is universally acknowledged, it would mean that, if we abandon them, we are abandoning the moral law.

On the Bolshevik side, Red China has often shown unequivocally that she quite clearly claims her place as leader in Asia. The last dramatic comparison between India and China came from the highest Communist ideological source when—significantly—the Soviet ambassador in Peking, Pavel Yudin, attacked the Indian Prime Minister Jawaharlal Nehru in the December (1958) issue of the revived journal of world Communism, *World Marxist Review*, which makes *ex cathedra* statements in Communist jargon in a dozen languages from Prague. In an article on 'The Basic Approach', published in 1958 in the paper of the Indian National Congress, *Economic Review*, on the occasion of Indian Independence Day (15th August), Nehru had condemned with reference to Gandhi's behaviour the Communist principle of the use of force and of ideology directed against personal freedom, and had emphasized that India, for her part, wanted to travel her own road to Socialism. Here he tried to clarify India's position between Capitalism and Communism. For his pains the Indian Pandit received a Communist lecture from 'Academician' Yudin. It was in fact the first condemnation of India from the highest Communist source since the death of Stalin, and was delivered in an extremely sharp manner. It was on the same old lines. No doubt it was the overture to an attack on all those who, by preserving an honourable neutrality and invoking the idea of *Panch-Shila* (which is even now being discredited in Peking), are unwilling to let themselves be overwhelmed by Communism.

We should understand this attack clearly. It fits into the conception of a new phase of power politics on the part of international Communism, drawn up by the twelve-power Eurasian Communist Convention in November 1957. If necessary, international Communism is to hasten political development in the Communist sense in any part of the world by means of revolutionary movements and armed pressure. One can imagine how repugnant such an attitude is to the Indian way of life, and to the idea of *Panch-Shila*, which is preached from the very spirit of India. It shows, however, that India, at this time of world conflict, has come more than any other country to occupy the key position in the decisions of the present. India will hold the balance of the free world in Asia, because the peoples of the Afro-Asian bloc look to her and are guided by her. In China Mao Tse-tung, who now dedicates himself only to rigid party ideology, once promised for propaganda purposes the 'thousand flowers' of liberal and broadminded thought, which, as Nehru regretted, soon 'became weeds to be torn out' and were petrified in the icy wind of Stalin's rising ideological storm. If this China were nevertheless to gain control of Asia's starving and begging masses, then freedom would be dead and buried in this greatest of continents, and our own freedom would be severely, too severely, curtailed. We in the 'West' should know that! We should understand Red China's forward surge by mobilizing its communes, which are regarded with mistrust even by the Soviet Russians and the European Communists; and we should understand India's world mission today. It is a question of destroying or protecting.

How near things can come to violence was shown in the Himalayan region in the territorial claim, by the People's Republic of China, for extensive areas in Ladakh and the North-Eastern Frontier Agency. China also put forward demands for alteration of the frontier in smaller areas of Uttar Pradesh, for instance, in the district of Nilang. The enormous areas which the Chinese army occupied were partly uninhabited, partly sparsely settled by small tribes. But these areas have strategic importance. Although the occupations dated back for some years, the Indians had not seen fit to make them public, perhaps in the belief that China itself would settle the matter amicably. But this is where New Delhi was mistaken. It was necessary to take defensive action against misleading Chinese maps, and to point out that the MacMahon Line was the traditional frontier in that Indo-Tibetan border region between Bhutan and Burma. But the Chinese declared that for them the findings of the Simla Conference had no significance.

It was not until 22nd April 1959 that the matter of Chinese military movements in the Almors District between the frontier posts of Taklakot and Bara Hoti were mentioned in the Indian

Parliament. The Indian public learned for the first time on 20th or 25th August 1959 that Chinese border guards had occupied Indian territory also in Ladakh, the West Tibetan part of the state of Kashmir and Jammu, and the North-Eastern Frontier Agency.

Since that time the presence of Chinese troops on territory traditionally recognized as Indian has brought Indo-Chinese relations to a dangerous state of tension. While it may seem incomprehensible to many Europeans on the one hand that Chinese soldiers should have occupied many thousands of square miles of Indian territory, and should be branded as aggressors, diplomatic relations between New Delhi and Peking have been maintained, though at a very frosty level, which the events of July 1962 on the mountain frontier have done nothing to improve.

Asia faces this choice—and we can only hope that insight is stronger than seductive words. India has shown herself to be a wise realist by accepting the political reality of Mao's state. But she knows where to draw the line: she has her own programme and her own path to follow. And the rest of Asia is not compelled to imitate. It needs merely to observe and to consider the programmes of its two greatest countries, between which a spiritual mountain soars up higher than the geographical Himalayas. And if Asia considers calmly and soberly, it might perhaps discover something for itself in India's way.

The senior priests of
Nepal

The monastery of Tashi-Lempo in the Tibetan district of Shigatse is the residence of the Panchen Lama

14

Philosophical and Political Epilogue

EVENTS IN THE HIMALAYAN REGION DEMAND AN ANSWER FROM THE WEST

OUR historical and political journey through the Himalayan region is ended. I hope I have been able to show the reader how here, in a wide area which will one day influence our future fate, thoughts ripened and kindled to historical deeds and then suddenly revealed themselves again in the iridescent garments of present-day politics. But every event was dependent on so many unreal factors, which made the situation appear even more complicated. We dare not ignore anything that happens in the Himalayas or in the vast region through which this mountain range runs like a powerful axis. Every event demands an answer from the West. Before we give an answer, however, we must ourselves clarify the situation and try to bring it into a wider historical perspective.

The alignment of the great empires of the world (including China), whose interests clash in only one geographical region, that is in the region of the Himalayas which we have been studying, has conjured up a dangerous situation through the accumulation of political power in two different centres of polarization. The neutral spectator states can do nothing to change the situation. Of the powers struggling for the world, the United States of America and their Western friends stand together with states on the so-called 'golden fringe of Asia' of which Lord Curzon once spoke; whilst the Soviet Russians and their Sino-Far-Eastern comrades in arms fighting for world revolutionary ends which demand more and more equality of rights in the Holy Empire of Marx, Engels, Lenin and Stalin, make sure of the heart of Asia, once regarded by the fathers of Anglo-Saxon geopolitics as a necessary condition for rule in Asia.

It was in the Himalayan region that ideas of world empire grew up. Philosophers dreamed here, and their influence was felt far away in the Western world. They were dreamers and yet clear thinkers; their thought grew up partly on the fringe of fantasy and philosophical-historical eclecticism, such as are found in the theosophical thoughts of the Russo-German Helene von Hahn, better known subsequently under the name of Helena Petrovna Blavatsky, who later presented from India to an 'astonished' world the *Holy Book of Dzyan*. Rulers reflected here on how to build peaceful empires, and even revolutionaries, concerned to improve the lot of their people, thought of eternal *Pax*, like that prophet of a peaceful kingdom of heaven upon earth who proclaimed a world paradise from China, as the Anabaptists once did from Münster in Westphalia. He was the leader of the Taiping rebellion, the simple muddled scholar Hung-Hsou-chuan, who had been converted to Christianity by a Protestant missionary, and who called his messianic universal kingdom *Tai Ping Tien Kuo* ('Great Heavenly Kingdom of Peace'). Here tribal princes mounted small, swift horses of the steppes, to hunt down kingdoms and crowns for themselves. And above all the cathedral of the spirit, prayed for and thought out by prophets and philosophers! Atheistic Utopians seek to tear it down. And Bolsheviks and Communists also use the beautifully simple, hopeful word 'peace' to conceal their lack of peace.

Two worlds came into collision here: ancient culture in the great Indo-Chinese area of river countries, where the longing for a *Pax universalis* always survived and found expression in universal kingdoms. In the Western, in the European part of the ancient cultural world this longing survived, too, ever since the *Imperium Romanum* had given the *Pax Romana* to the world. And we experienced in great measure a modern East-West revival of the experiment made by Alexander the Great, when the *Pax Britannica* shone out from India over the border territories of the Indian Ocean. Today, in the same area, India is proclaiming her kingdom of peace. It could be called *Shanti Raj*.

If the striving in the conservative peasant states of Asia was an imperial struggle of the 'Chakravartin', who later transferred the idea of this Western imperialism into the sphere of religion, in conceptions of a kingdom of peace, the tendency towards the universal was controlled by a humanity illuminated by divine commandments. On the other hand, the impulses from the steppe lands were immeasurable and unlimited, but they too were still wedded to faith. Once again today universal thoughts seek universal aims on the soil of universal empires. However, only in combination with the secular materialism and atheistic lack of restraint is this universal dream a danger and a brutal reality which the present masters of the steppe lands, the Muscovite dictators of Eurasia, want to achieve over the whole earth, in the world revolutionary struggle for Asia.

Anyone who is studying this contested Asia should begin his spiritual journey in Russia. The unique phenomenon of Russia, once the traditional representative of Byzantine imperialism and devotional faith on the stage of world history, is that she dedicated herself to those ideas which sought to force the realization of conceptions of world empire from the Mongolian steppes. And the gospel of a Christian Third Rome, once proclaimed and sought after in ardent suffering by the Pleskau monk, Philoteus, allied itself to a secular Mongolian lust for conquest, which, however, still bore traces of religious feeling. Long ago the Turkish Mongolian Khans marked, on their sand-drawn maps of the countries and kingdoms thought suitable for conquest, the points of attack by means of golden apples, called *Kizil Elma* (Alma-Ata—father of the apples—is still today the name of Kazakstan's capital). In the same way the Soviet heirs of Asiatic Mongolian dynamism seek out their modern 'golden apples' today. They mingled Byzantine universality with this Mongolian dynamism, putting on in addition the garment of Christianity and assuming a demoniacal robe foreshadowed by Dostoyevsky. Material urges and holy aspirations were falsified into brutal means to attain the Communist end. Such stages as revolutions, revolts and strikes are to lead to it. And the fighters for world supremacy are no longer to be found at the barriers, but sit at the planning centres of a world conflagration. The Third Rome became the Third International, that international Communism which would like to establish the dictatorship of the proletariat over the whole world by means of a force which only now and then allows itself a tactical respite.

Today two powers hold the balance of world political strength in their hands. The first of them received it full of amazement, when still wrapped in dreams of isolationism. This was the United States of America. Uncomplicated as the heroes of their films, who are well known to us, they seized power and let fall the curtains of isolationist seclusion. And when this happened they spoke of crusades and new world peace organizations. Yet their 'uncomplicatedness' was honourable—and unsound, and their opposite numbers were as unscrupulous as they were full of noisy propaganda. But facing the godless Third Rome stood a new power, a new Rome. This American New Rome tried to build a new empire of harmony for all peoples, the United Nations Organization. It was as though the blazing thoughts of the German democrats Karl Göpp and Theodor Pösche of the 1848 revolution had been realized in America. They had formulated their plans for world peace in 1852 in a document *E pluribus unum* and in 1853 in the propaganda work *The New Rome, or the United States of the World.* On 29th January 1852 their American Revolutionary League for Europe had called upon Europeans from Philadelphia, the Anglo-German Quaker city, to unite in a universal world republic. Europe was still the 'pivot of history'. Meanwhile a restless feeling of stress, a violent revolt and the will to freedom permeates the many-coloured world. The 'victory of colonial peoples' is proclaimed. It is the eternal change in the course of history, known even to the Roman poet Horace, for otherwise one of his distichs would not have been able to tell of the victory of *Graecia capta* over victorious Rome. But a hundred years after the call from America the great-great grandchildren of those planners, disillusioned by the tragedy of the League of Nations and the failure of the United Nations Organization, warned the Europeans to form an alliance in order to save themselves. And an ocean named after the mysterious Atlantis became the link between the Atlantic nations. The Atlantic community was proclaimed, the league of maritime nations. Meanwhile the Himalayas became the axis of continental lands, yesterday still living in colonial or semi-colonial status. Maritime endeavour develops individualism. The Promethean, Faustian will of the West once forced its way into world history on the shores of the Aegean and finally freed itself from the maternal cultural heritage of Asia in a sea battle—at Salamis. Asia, even in the culturally profuse border territories, is oppressed by the weight of the continental mass, and the magnet is the Himalayas. The Atlantic and the Himalayas are like symbolic manifestations in space of the historical east-west dialectic. The historical tensions and contradictions, which can manifest themselves in such different ways as Europe against Asia, or Eurasia against the fringe of Asia, suddenly appear close and tangible when they are projected into a geographical reality.

The continental attacks against maritime countries and against the cultural area of the passively maritime regions of the fringe of Asia were caused by the dynamism of land—and food-hungry tribes, or were just expressions of strength. Today this dynamic power has measured itself against the strength of the Christian faith, has drawn from it divine unity and developed into a secular atheistic social religion, which, like the medieval geographical division of *Sacerdotium*, *Imperium* and *Studium*, forces doctrine, power and textual interpretation towards one central point— Moscow.

However, after brief attempts to reinterpret the only true doctrines of the four Communist evangelists, Marx, Engels, Lenin and Stalin (made by political opportunists but shocking to the orthodox) the 'First Moscow' saw a 'Second Moscow' arise in the Imperial Palace in Peking. Here the guardians of the sacred yet so ungodly writings are even more Muscovite than the people on the Moskva. There is also the fact that certain political realities, such as the existence of Outer Mongolia, are a blow to Chinese pride. But Peking's multifarious and over-hasty programme of industrialization still demands, both economically and politically, a strong association with the Kremlin. Moreover, the American policy of 'quarantine' makes this necessary.

The drive of this Communist world, with its simple, clearly defined ideas, is directed with an aggressive energy which manifests itself in boastful propaganda from the Soviet Union, and with somewhat greater dialectic (drawing a veil over the repetition of the Hungarian tragedy in Tibet and starting its encroachment into the Himalayas with paper annexations on falsified maps) from the Chinese People's Republic, into the southern Himalayan region and from there to the whole area which we regard today as the playground of Afro-Asian forces. And from here propaganda by means of radio and the printed word is addressed to the world of South and Central America, where the mixture of Red Indian, Negroid and partly Indian blood is certain to attract Afro-Asian sympathy. The Communist bastion of propaganda and revolutionary movement is, however, Turkestan, the country which is so important in the present struggle for Afro-Asian friendship. From a propaganda point of view it is the roof of the world. And from the political and geographical viewpoint which is expanded here, one passes to the theological and recalls that Augustine long ago saw the eschatological struggle approaching from the 'roof', meaning, however, as Jerome explains and Augustine also reports, the much disputed Bible word *Gog* ('roof') and *Magog* ('from the roof'). Both symbolize manifestations and forces which as atheistic leaders attack God's people.

Mention of purely symbolic conceptions of power leads naturally to the question of the future historical development of the area with which we are concerned. The question cannot be answered at a theoretical distance. Because of our own involvement in the area—as in every other area of our shrunken earth—we are compelled to give a conscientious answer. But this answer has to be stretched to cover the whole of the globe—that is the lesson of this very region where thought always tended towards the whole, towards the universal. The struggle of our time is the global battle between powers who hold such infinitely different philosophical and political views of the world, and seek to control it from their very dissimilar standpoints. The universality which Hegel saw in the spirit of understanding, and which Marx defined in the classless society (unworldly and yet at the same time moving worldly people more), has been interpreted in our time by Toynbee as a universal religion, which he sees as the last signpost and as the sign of victory over our declining civilization. One may not accept the form of Toynbee's conceptions, but he understood that in the last resort the struggle for the world is a religious one. It is the battle between religions of salvation acknowledging God and the secular Communist social religion. To know of salvation upon earth—that is the Christian interpretation, and the believers in God of all creeds are often Christians in the Augustinian sense in their similar philosophies. ('In illa ineffabili providentia Dei multi, qui foris videntur, intus sunt, et multi, qui intus videntur, foris sunt', Augustine writes by way of interpretation in his work, *De baptismo contra Donatistas*.) Our historic task has one aim only: our fulfilment. A Christian is he who, full of confidence, sees the true future beyond the darkness of the present. But unfortunately amidst the insecurity of our time, many have lost the compass of confidence which makes possible their orientation to a single goal, to God. If that goal is there, we can be surrounded by emptiness, and even in the void of the present we can still find a place where the spheres of intimacy, of personal intercourse, and of prayer are preserved. Only then—and the believers of the East should tell the believers and the unbelievers of the West—can we proceed to solve the individual problems of our time. Unfortunately our scientific knowledge, ever hunting and pressing forward to new horizons, enflames us atheistically, to be 'completely uncommitted'. It lost its shining roof and was split—and spiritual and material atomic fission was the result. This was also the case in branches of knowledge which—like that of history—should have given a universal picture of the earth. Only now, when we can feel once more the breath of religiosity (in the sciences too), is universality restored to us. A new era had followed the spiritual world of Augustine's *Civitas Dei* up to Bossuet's *Discours sur l'histoire universelle*, but it soon spent itself in stress and endeavour. Today our task is to preserve the new trend which is at last leading us to contemplate things and events as a whole. This contemplation can find a direction which is finally satisfying only through faith in the community of men and in their divine mission. Here alone is the starting-point for the final solution of all our problems, large and small.

Knowledge of the Himalayan region, which in itself—especially as regards the southern parts—scarcely bears the urgency of historical truth, should convince us that it is necessary to allow ourselves to be guided not by an egocentricity like that of existentialism, but only by a general perspective. Thus if we want to judge correctly and to help really decisively, we must start from the highest principles of faith, that is to say, they must find their centre of salvation outside the human sphere with its subjection to the personal. After this restless age, which by its technical achievements is depriving us of our last intimate reserves, it is only in the field of metaphysics that man will finally achieve that peace which can lead to a renaissance of humanity.

We can change the world only if this rebirth is accompanied by love and courageous confidence in the individual. This personal spiritual event, this appeal to the individual, has undergone a reinterpretation in the Communist process of revaluation, leading finally to compulsory self-criticism *coram publico*; thus it became nothing more than a means of oppressing the individual. Here I should like to quote from Jack Belden, the American author of the book, *China Shakes the World*. Belden, who is not at all unsympathetic towards the Communists, writes with admiration about the 'achievements' but unconsciously shows also the reverse of the medal:

In times of troubles, when prophets spring up, people have a great desire to start life all over again, to wash away both the sins and the sorrows of the past. This idea of rebirth is a strong motive force behind the Communist drive in China. It has nothing in common with Chiang Kai-shek's New Life Movement which concerned itself with external things like keeping one's clothes buttoned or not spitting on the streets. It goes much deeper than that and touches some of the inner chords of men.

The biggest slogan of the Chinese Communists has been 'Fan Shen' (literally, 'to turn over the body', but sometimes translated as 'standing on your own feet'). When applied to politics 'Fan Shen' means to overturn the landlord system, overturn feudalism, overturn dictatorship. But 'Fan Shen' is more than this. It is a distinct and conscious effort to give the Chinese a moral ethic. When applied to the individual, it means to overturn your thoughts, overturn your way of life, overturn your conscience. The philosophy behind such an ethic is of course the philosophy of reform, but it goes even deeper than that, for it embraces the idea of rebirth also.

Another aspect of 'Fan Shen' lies in the longing that everyone has to recapture his youth. In times of political and social reawakening, a whole race may be afflicted with the desire to rediscover its childhood. At such periods, forgotten folk ways, dances, songs and traditions froth to the surface again. So it has been that the Chinese people have taken the revived *Yangko* songs and dances to their hearts and gone swinging in chanting conga lines down the streets of all the villages and cities in North and Central China. The Communists in this way have satisfied popular yearnings to dance, to laugh, to be carefree once again.

Because group songs and group dances are an expression of a collective spirit as opposed to an individualistic spirit, they always furnish a revolutionary power which bases itself on the 'people'—a ready field for propaganda. Singing and dancing have definitely been weapons in building up Communist power and also in creating a fraternal feeling among the masses. . . .

Closely allied with the idea of rebirth is the idea of salvation. The appeal here is on several different planes. One is: 'You are doomed; but there is a way out.' This is the revolutionary appeal, the redemption of all mankind through the class struggle. The words 'class struggle', however, were seldom used by the Chinese Communists in their dealings with the people. The appeal was much more basic and simple than that. It was a case of telling the people: 'You are starving, save yourself, band together, join us.'

Salvation was also to be achieved by 'self-purification'. The 'broken shoe' was to purify herself of lustful emotions, the intellectual to purge himself of snobbish thoughts, the landlord to chase greed out of his heart, the peasant to rid himself of slothfulness, the cadre member to purify himself night and day of the 'dogmatic way of handling affairs'.

The road to salvation was not easy, but there was a guide—the People's Army and the Communist Party. This thought is well expressed by the title of a song, 'You are my Lighthouse'. The party thus inculcated the idea that it was the shepherd of the people.

To the evil members of society, the Communists promised salvation through repentance. Husbands should repent for their treatment of their wives, landlords for their bad treatment of tenants, the Kuomintang for the treatment of the people and even the 'imperialists' for their treatment of China.

Repentance does not seem to be an idea original with the Communists, for it was also used by the Kuomintang. . . .

The last sentence must be slightly corrected, for self-criticism was not introduced under the Kuomintang until the twenties, when a brief flirtation began between Canton and the Communists in the Kremlin. The longing to be *homo novus* is found in all ideologies and all spiritual movements. How vital is the way to this new man and what purpose he has to serve! The religion of Christ was unique in awakening the social conscience of the West —and thereby of modern humanity in general!—and in creating Europe, a continent better understood through its anthropological and spiritual history than as a geographical continent; this religion has boldly blended the material and the spiritual through its knowledge of the personal God. Christianity has left the bed of its religion and has sent forth streams of its spirit into all directions of the religious world. It could therefore be broadly conceived in the Augustinian sense to have caused Gandhi (influenced by Thoreau and Tolstoy) to make a unique Christian experiment having its deepest roots in Christ's Sermon on the Mount.

Only if we face the conditions of the present with the equanimity of a faith effective even in a vacuum (that is the product of all philosophical and historical meditation), and if we estimate the human and political danger zones of our time from this tranquil point of view, can we disentangle the numerous knots of problems which have many sides and many layers.

One of the great questions of our modern world is undoubtedly that of the independence of states and their peoples. Will they go the way of the communities of white ants, where every thought and act is prescribed for them, and will they finally, creatures without will-power like the lemmings, plunge themselves into the abyss of soullessness and dehumanization? The problem of freedom is concerned. The philosopher Hegel, who reinterpreted the dialectical system of Thesis—Antithesis—Synthesis (more real than ever today) as the logical process of world history, said in his lectures on 'Reason in History':

> The Orientals do not know that the spirit of man as such is free in himself. Because they do not know this they are not free. They only know that One is free, but for that very reason such freedom is only caprice, wildness, insensibility of the emotions or just a mildness and tameness of freedom, which is itself merely an accident of nature or a caprice. This One is therefore a despot, not a free man, a human being.

Hegel sees the edifice of the human race as a hierarchy at the head of which stand the representatives of the state. But is not the state, for the majority of Asiatics, something strange, inimical, something to be avoided? The surprising thing is that in contrast to the philosophical views of Hegel and of modern interpreters of Asiatic despotism, the people of Asia are in reality much freer because of their anti-state mentality. The *staretz* in Old Russia (which in this connection I should like to count as the East), the *swami*, *sadhu* and *bhikkhu* of Asia were extreme forms of free men. It was not until after contact with Western civilization that the type of beggar known to us became also a general phenomenon here in Asia. Indifference also has another result. It made people indifferent to the overthrowing of the state, to *coups d'état* and revolutions. These have always been the concern of small classes or groups. The wave of military dictatorships in the non-Communist belt of Asia—e.g. in Iraq, Burma, Pakistan, Thailand—proves it. It is misleading to compare here the interim period of dictatorships in Europe—that is, in the East European states. But both have two things in common: the desire to remain nationally independent, and not to be crushed by the steam-roller of Bolshevik Eurasia.

The Western task in the countries of Asia and the regions of Africa can only be not to show partiality for one régime or one person but to try to gain closer contact even with politically indifferent populations. We have at our disposal so many means of explanation, help and construction, which we should not simply give but should distribute so that everybody knows about them. The people in the villages should not be forgotten either. What the men and women of the (North) American Technical Co-operation Mission are doing (without many words) in the Indian villages is a shining example in this respect. If we send out such advisers of the people, who do not serve cliques but become protectors of national aspirations, we shall easily build in these lands a Himalaya of confidence and self-assurance. Then healthy forces will stir. Let it be our aim not to defame them but to help their growth. Asia trusts us. We should also trust Asia.

15

Where is the World Stage?

SPECTATORS AND ACTORS SHARE THE
SAME FATE

TODAY every event anywhere in the world concerns every one of
us, for we are inhabitants of one planet. The world has suddenly
shrunk. Sparks anywhere in Asia can easily set fire to houses in
Europe, America or Australia, or can burn down the huts of
Africa.

In the most complicated area on earth the huge arch of the
Himalayan range has become as it were the proscenium of current
history. We do not yet know where the stage is; it may be to the
north or to the south. It depends upon the biological strength of
the nations and on the power of their convictions. We know only
one thing: the actors and spectators in this game of world politics
may be far apart but their fate is the same. With inexorable consistency Nature has added total experience to the total thirst for
knowledge of the West and the total intoxication with power of
the Eurasians, who have taken over from the Asiatic heritage the
conception of totality and from the Western heritage the urge to
win and acquire things.

The times demand, therefore, a revolutionary rethinking, or at
least deep reflection. The old clothes are no use; we must give the
world new ones. First of all, in a new general view of the world,
which in technical experiments is already pursuing cosmic plans,
but in the political sphere is still moving at the same snail's pace,
priority must be given to a synthesis of thought. Let us not conceal
it: the panacea of an age which still understood how to play with

162

power like skilled fencers was the policy of *divide et impera*. Even today 'division' is one of the most frequently used political words. From Germany to Korea and Vietnam there are divided states whose reunion by means of a simple, reasonable solution is vetoed by the ideological cramp of one side.

But in the non-Communist area there are also countries which are divided and in which the great powers then generally show favour to one of the two successor states. It is dangerous. The Western programme should be a bold policy of synthesis.

The West should reconsider the whole subcontinent of India from this point of view, and should propose to the nations a unified economic *modus vivendi* which would lead to the weakening of political contrasts and territorial demands. Of course the nations have to determine their own territories, but nobody will oppose a thoughtful and peaceful policy of making proposals.

Similarly, bold experiments are needed in the Middle East, where a synthesis between Arabs and Israelis can alone prevent genocide. In the long run a solution of the problems of North Africa will be found only in a federation of the three Arab-Berber countries. An Aegean Federation with Constantinople as capital would strengthen the position in the eastern Mediterranean. Is it not possible that a policy of synthesis might also be helpful in the supranational and economic spheres—for example, by the formation of a World Oil Union on the lines of the European Coal and Steel Community? The profits would then benefit the whole of the Middle East, and after the expansion of the Indian oilfields in Assam and the development of new fields near Cambay the area which we have been discussing here would also be affected. The Antarctic Treaty is already a political decision which will condemn purely national interest in the White Continent.

The words 'policy of synthesis' may seem to many people a slogan of Utopian character. In the national framework it may sound like lazy compromise between parties. But in world politics it is after all in the age of the atom bomb the only hope of salvation for that part of the world which has not yet fallen under the Communist yoke. Synthesis in the free area is the answer to compulsory union in the Communist territories. The call to synthesis—here meant as a spiritual union of understanding and nothing more—in mutual consideration and respectful tolerance is also the challenge in the religious world, where the state of affairs on both sides of the Communist frontiers is only a world-wide diaspora.

We in the 'West' are today paying for our 'colonialism' with interest. (I do not want to argue here about the true meaning of the word, and about the good and bad sides of this economic and political encounter between nations!) Here we should not become resigned to the inevitable, but with the payments should ensure new credit for ourselves today. The peoples of Asia and Africa are not only thirsting for the springs of political and national freedom. They also want to share the fleshpots and rice-bowls of economic and technical progress. The Soviet Union, still regarded with mistrust as a Western technical country at the time of the Bandung Conference, is, since the Suez crisis, significantly regarded as the protagonist of an anti-colonial war of liberation. It is of no importance whether this war against colonialism is in fact a tilting at windmills, a policy of 'Stop, thief!', because the real colonialists in Asia are the Russians, with a colonialism of populations such as was never practised by West European nations on Asian soil. The important thing is to imagine the feelings of the Asians and to react accordingly. Therefore it is satisfactory that the West has overcome its reluctance to give aid for development to Asian countries; and the great annual meeting of the World Bank and the International Monetary Fund from 6th to 10th October 1958 may be taken as documentary proof of the readiness of world finance (that means the West) to grant credit. That was an answer which might help to stabilize the position in non-Communist Asia. From Communist Asia distress signals flash from time to time across the Formosa straits. Peking's Communist Central Committee presses nervously onwards and compels the Soviet 'big brother' to take decisions with which he cannot whole-heartedly agree.

The struggle for Asia is reaching a decisive stage. Are we psychologically armed? In the last few years thousands of Asian students and apprentices have passed through Western universities and factories. Here the question arises as to how the students are cared for, and what sort of after-care they receive. Simply to dismiss the young Asians without concerning oneself further in any way about their fate is short-sightedness and stupidity. Further concern means still to regard them in some way or other as members of the Western universities and therefore to maintain continuous contact with them as former students. Concern for the young people from Asia and Africa begins with their arrival in the Western host country. In my book, *India-Pakistan-Ceylon*, which appeared in 1956, I suggested the foundation of an Afro-Asian University in the Federal Republic of Germany. Then I saw in Tashkent the great Central Afro-Asian University, which is a kind of Afro-Asian Technical College of Communism. What I saw confirmed me in my view of the necessity of founding such a university in my country also, where, unlike Tashkent, Afro-Asian students should be introduced to Western intellectual thought and free Western research. The same ideas moved me in Tashkent's Navoi Library, a collection founded in 1870 and equipped with two million books, one of the greatest treasures of Asia. Since 1948 it has borne the name of the late medieval Uzbek poet Alisher Navoi. There too I met students from various parts of Asia. (I should like to mention here that I was shown, as one of the greatest treasures of the library, the first Bible printed in Nürnberg in 1483 by Anton Koberger, and similarly a copy of Ulrich von Hutten's Latin works with a personal dedication to the Count Palatine.) I do not want to expound my plan again here, but I may perhaps draw attention to a commentary on it which appeared in the *dpa-Letter/Culture* on 18th January 1957. The point of view emphasized by Ernst Berger is somewhat as follows:

. . . the informative book on the Indian region tries to give a view of the different aspects of Indian life and is also specially concerned with fostering cultural relations between Germany and the Indian sub-continent. Here the author is led to speak of a new form of cultural relations which seem to him to be a worthwhile aim for our efforts:

'Germany's efforts to find more and more points of contact in Indian cultural life need to be fostered with loving care. Germany, whose scientists and poets, and more recently merchants and technicians, forged such strong links between the two cultural worlds, should create in her own country a great centre specially concerned with these countries which today feel themselves more and more involved in a common Afro-Asian fate. Germany particularly could give the peoples of Asia and Africa the possibility of bringing their knowledge up to date and training themselves in German science. This is both a huge cultural undertaking and a political task. The possibility could be offered through a kind of university for foreigners, that is, the foundation of an Afro-Asian University on German soil. Probably no city in Germany is better adapted for this purpose than Stuttgart, where because of the many foreign scientific institutes, the right atmosphere for a meeting of foreign nations has existed for long enough. The link between such a university, at which public offices like the Federation and private ones like management could take over a great task, and the already existing technical college, would perhaps produce a new and happy type of student. The realization of such a plan should be a cultural aim.'

International cultural relations have assumed a new form, particularly between the highly industrialized and the so-called underdeveloped countries. Offers of scholarships are playing an ever-increasing part. After Nehru's visit the Indian Prime Minister was able to take home with him a generous gift: the German guarantee of 712 scholarships. It must not be overlooked that in addition hundreds of scholarship-holders come to Germany in other ways. German industry knows that it cannot remain indifferent to the question of scholarships.

All these offers of scholarships, which partly also signify an industrial training, have been made so far somewhat involuntarily. A cautious adjustment and also a certain amount of regulation would be necessary here.

But the most important thing may well be the reflection that all the Afro-Asian students come from a cultural world which has a completely different social structure. These young people are largely members of a world in which the family decides and controls everything, in which the sexes are strictly separated from one another, and in which the way of life in general is far removed from ours. Simply to put these students down in the midst of the free, uninhibited European world without any further kindly and responsible guidance can have severe psychological consequences for these young people. It should not be forgotten that even in European states such as Italy there are universities for foreigners which are intended for European students, as, for example, Perugia. In France, Grenoble performs a similar task. But what here seemed fitting for European students is gradually becoming an urgent necessity in our country for young people from Asia and Africa.

In such a university for foreigners, which would be equipped with students' hostels, it would not be necessary to give the students large sums of money as scholarships. It should not be overlooked that very many students and trainees in Germany receive on average about 300 marks (£27 5s. 0d.) a month. In India that is about 350 rupees—a fine sum, the equivalent of the salary of the best-paid professor in India after ten years of teaching activity. If on the other hand the students were granted free accommodation and free tuition, and in addition received a small but adequate amount of pocket money, then the breach with their past in their own families would not be nearly so great, and the damage which can be done would be almost eliminated.

These are only a few of the reasons which can be discussed with all

The place where Buddha found enlightenment, the Bô-tree

publicity. But they should be sufficient to show how desirable it can be both for the givers and the receivers if the plan for such an Afro-Asian university were to be boldly tackled in Germany.

At the moment I will add no more to this commentary on my proposal.

Our next move in Germany should be to promote an 'Asia Society'; but I have already indicated this in my book, *Asia— Continent of Decision*.

The distribution of real knowledge about Asia, more especially from the viewpoint of qualified psychologists, is a stern necessity, because more and more people from the West are going there for professional reasons and making long stays. Unfortunately the psychological aspect is very often neglected. We often believe that good administrative or technical knowledge—or whatever the province may be—should suffice. That is not true, and therefore the selection for Asia at all levels of officials sent by the civil service or private firms should take into consideration the psychological and human side. Let us not fall into the error of regarding everything from the point of view of technical, industrial or any other kind of appropriateness. Let us just consider the formality so much respected in various parts of Asia and unfortunately often not respected by the adherents of a free and easy type of Americanism. Let us hear what a Japanese, Sugaware Yoshimasa, has to say on this point in his book, *They are Watching Us—a Diary of Our Time*:

Even in war Kitayama does not want to renounce the spirit of 'formality'. Whilst he was in the U.S.A. nothing was more painful to him and he found nothing more incomprehensible than the informality there. Were people so strong spiritually and intellectually, so uninhibited, that they could afford to do it, he pondered even then, or was it only the expression of their childlike awkwardness and way of kicking over the traces? Later in China he had found, however, that the Americans whom he met were mostly very practical people who should not be underestimated. Therefore he wanted to make the effort to learn what was good from them. Not more. Not the rest.

Now, many Asians try to get to know strangers, and especially those who can easily be defamed by malevolent propaganda. Finally, the Asians have nevertheless gradually understood that Americanism is in no way a concealed form of colonialism, and that informality has nothing to do with scorn for foreign manners

M

and disrespect towards Asian customs, as skilfully directed propaganda was able to blare out.

Whilst we in the West—no more stupid words have wormed their way so deeply into the political vocabulary of the present than geographical designations for spiritual, political and cultural spheres—whilst we in the West have to deal with these small details of our psychological attitude, the Russians are acting in a big way. We forget that one should not only give (the West has gradually realized this!), but that one must also say that one has done it. Explanation is necessary. But explanation and information, which are used partially as a political means, are propaganda. We despise propaganda, and rightly so. But is that a reason for not going the right way to work with our friends in Asia and planning things which are after all meant only for them? In 1957 the Russians put on the great Indo-Soviet film *Pardesi* ('The Stranger'), which was to portray to the Indians on gay-coloured celluloid the life of the Russian traveller Afanasi (Athanasius) Nikitin in the fifteenth century. This chance traveller became a pioneer of Russo-Indian friendship, and history was reinterpreted into the epic of a traditionally heartfelt meeting between the two peoples. On the other hand the West, represented by the dream-factory of Hollywood, offers to the young people of India, who come from a completely different environment, nothing but horror stories from gangster worlds which are but grist to the Communist mills. There are many Western film companies which take credit from the state. Could not a few suggestions be given with the credit? There must be so many East-West themes available that someone should just take up! Why do we not think of simply crediting East-West societies with millions for such purposes, as trustees for relations between East and West? They will pay more dividends than the most thrilling story from Hollywood. The countries of Asia are building up internal political systems which, in accordance with the character of the state, simply cannot do without a certain amount of planning. In the case of some of our exports, we should ask what is the purpose and sense of them, and we should keep some check on those people who are sensationally chasing after money. In matters of enlightenment, in the difficult questions of cultural policy—the accent is on the first of these words—we should rise above the daily round of routine work and set about some generous planning, seek world-wide goals long since made attainable through technical and economic progress. Is it because they have to stand upon the feet of private enterprise? Nothing is more dangerous than mediocrity allied with power—a threatening sign for our time, which is so poor in an élite. But this is the good fortune of Soviet Russia, who by dictatorially swift deeds can make the actions of the West seem like a policy of clumsy fencing, sadly lacking in ideas.

But let us not linger here over particular details. The history of the Himalayan region challenges the present, and it gleams at the bottom of the glittering goblets of politics. The riddle of the present struggle in the world, which is probably most clearly seen on both sides of the Himalayan ridge, can only be answered from the point of view of universal history. And here in the Himalayas is the universe: magic, at home in the lamaseries, jostles with metaphysics which are given a pantheistic interpretation or perhaps are based on Thomas Aquinas or Aristotle; and myth, nourished in the emotional worlds of political dreamers and philosophizing historians, stands suddenly next to a clear interpretation of existence dictated by reason. In this region of contacts where Aryans or Indo-Europeans and Ural-Altaians had their original home in present-day Turan, where people look for Paradise, the Eden of Adam and Eve, history is announcing a world drama. We have to discover whether there is tragedy in the drama. The drama of our time, which has discovered a psychoanalysis of the theatre, where spectators and actors unite in common action, demands participation from everybody, the people on the stage and the people in front of it. The dramatic events in the Himalayas unite spectators and actors. On this knowledge we should base our attitude towards this political problem. We should not forget that the actor performing on Asia's stage, set in the mountains of the gods, is humanity itself.

INDEX

INDEX

Figures in **bold type** in the entry refer to the pages of the chapter where a country or an item is treated at some length.

173

70

70
71
72
74
75
76
77
79
80
88